Girls LEAD

EXTRAORDINARY GIRLS SHARE HOW YOU CAN STAND UP, STEP OUT AND LEAD IN ALL AREAS OF YOUR LIFE!

Introduction by Julie Carrier

Recognized as America's #1 Speaker for Girls

Authored By Extraordinary Girls and Young Women

Positive
Role Model Press

www.beyoutifulclub.com

© 2017 by Julie Speaks, Inc.
ISBN: 978-0-615-88161-4

Published by Positive Role Model Press
www.beyoutifulclub.com

Printed in the United States of America.

Cataloging-in-Publication Data is on file with the Library of Congress.

Contents

Introduction

_By_
Julie Carrier

Girls Lead!
You...LEAD!

How do I know?

    As an award-winning speaker recognized as "America's #1 Speaker for Girls," a young women's success coach for an Emmy-Award winning TV show, the author of BeYOUtiful! and a go-to expert on the "girl world"—and as someone who has reached nearly a million girls, women and young people across the globe—I feel fortunate that I get to see the truth of this nearly every day!

I see girls, like you, boldly leading movements for positive change. Girls *lead*!

I see girls, like you, who step up to start their own campaigns to end bullying, reduce poverty, promote positive choices, and so many other important causes. Girls *lead*!

I see girls, like you, determined to overcome tough times and use their struggles to help others make it through their own challenging times. Girls *lead*!

I see girls, like you, who generously help underserved kids in the U.S. and other countries and who raise thousands of dollars for charity. Girls *lead*!

I see girls, like you, bravely stand up for what is right, even when they feel they have to stand alone. Girls *lead*!

I see that *every girl*, like you, already has an amazing leader inside of them—and I know, whether you feel it or not right now, you already *are* a leader and you *already* have everything you need within you to truly lead and succeed! The key is being able to let that amazing leader shine brighter!

But it's not always easy. Many girls, who want to let their leader shine, often feel alone. Why? Because, sadly—and you may agree—the many amazing examples of other girls and women leading can sometimes be hard to focus on in a world overshadowed by tons of negative media hype painting a very different picture of what matters. Often the heroic stories, the inspiring messages and the powerful examples of girls and women leaders are not even a tiny whisper in a media environment that seems to shout constantly about the latest Reality TV Star's trip cat fights, mean girl drama, and publicity stunts involving not-so-great choices. What's up with that?!?! It makes me want to swap my favorite smiley emoji with the really angry one! No, seriously—it makes me want to take action!

In fact, I'm so passionate about helping girls and women, I even left my job as a Senior Management Consultant in Leadership Training and Development for the Pentagon. While I taught and developed interactive education and brain-based leadership programs for executives at the Pentagon, I kept thinking about where I had started in middle school and high school—an awkward girl who had crippling anxiety, self doubt—and who saw herself as anything but a leader.

At that time, like many girls, all those negative media messages quickly turned my "girls can lead" attitude into "girls just can't." Based upon what I was hearing and seeing in magazines, music, online and on TV, I felt awkward, like an outsider—like there was something wrong with me. Because I cared about trying to be my best and about being a leader, I felt like I didn't fit in with all the hype of what I "should be." I felt like I needed to hide my smarts and "dumb myself down," blend in instead of stand out, hide my positive choices instead of be proud of them, and generally hide my potential as a leader.

Then, later during my freshman year of high school, I saw a powerful speaker who was invited to my school. Hearing the message, I was so inspired! I realized, for the first time, that I could be a confident leader and stand up to share my message to inspire others. I began to see my entire future and myself differently!

It didn't stop there! My experience seeing this positive role model and speaker at my school inspired me to look for and see other amazing role models through what I chose to read, who I chose to listen to, and the mentors that I found.

My old thoughts of "girls just can't" quickly began to transform into "maybe girls can" and then "girls *can* lead—and *absolutely do!*" I was no longer the shy and awkward teen who listened to negative media hype. What I saw and heard from my *positive* role models and their *positive* messages inspired me to do so many things!! Their examples and encouragement helped me start my own successful business as an entrepreneur at the age of 14 to earn money for college; run for and become elected as Junior Class Vice President and National Honor Society President; be selected as a National Century III Leader as one of the top 50 student leaders in the nation; earn a Rotary Ambassadorial Scholarship to England and serve as a representative of international goodwill and understanding...it even brought me all the way to the Pentagon where I was hired as a Senior Management Consultant in Leadership Development at the age of just 23.

When I thought about how far I'd come and all the amazing women who had helped and inspired me along the way, I realized it was time to give back! Because I also saw so many girls who were treading water or struggling in a sea of misleading role models and media messages, I knew that now was the time to help change things—so I launched my new role to serve as an international advocate, author, and speaker for girls and women on leadership who has reached more than a million world-wide.

Now I'm not saying all this to impress you, I'm saying this to impress upon you that, if I can lead a life more incredible than I could have ever imagined, with a "Girls Lead" attitude, so can you! (Now my life is far from perfect, but a "Girls Lead" attitude can help us create the up times in life and get through the really tough down times, too!)

I'm grateful and honored that my messages have been so well received—by girls and parents; by leading girls organizations like Girl Scouts, Girls on The Run, Young Women Lead, Girls Inc., women's conferences, and sororities; and at student leadership events and in my BeYOUtiful® Conferences held in small towns and large cities alike across America—yet, *still* my attempts to bring more positive programming and messages for and about girls to the *media* airwaves was met with a very different response. I've been told repeatedly by some in the media elite—from New York to LA—(to quote one agent directly) "You are 'too good' for TV. Character and positive values don't sell. We have no interest in representing you, your show, or your messages."

Too "good" for TV? Seriously?!? So basically he was telling me that girls across the world like you reading this book should *not* be represented in the media because we care about making good choices and trying to be our best?!? We don't deserve to hear or see messages on positive character, body-confidence and leadership? Does that make any sense? No! For some in the media, their focus on catfights, conflict and poor choices may make dollars from ratings, yes, but it doesn't make sense for us! What is the *real* cost to girls, to how they see themselves and their futures?

No wonder that the unrepresented majority—real girls in the real world, like you, who want to stand up as leaders or make a difference in their lives and the lives of others—often feel alone, or like outsiders, or like they don't fit in.

That's why, with your help, we are starting to change things!

How? Because of the support of some amazing girls like you, parents, professionals, organizations, and companies who care about promoting a positive message of leadership for girls, I'm leading a movement across the country and the globe to provide girls positive, uplifting messages, programs, and conference experiences—much-needed positive alternatives to so much of the negative media hype.

Why are we doing this? Because you are NOT alone—and you deserve to live in a world where you feel valued, you feel you belong, you love who you are (and your body the way it is), and you feel supported in leading your boldest, brightest and best life possible!

I'm humbled that my messages for girls—spoken live on some of the largest stages around the country in my keynote programs and delivered in books like this one in your hands, or in best-practice curricula, on-line programs, and positive TV shows around the world—are applauded by an army of tens of thousands of girls, women, teens, parents and professionals! We celebrate and applaud a different type of girl—far from Reality TV drama stereotypes. I'm talking about a *real* girl for the *real* world—a girl who stands for leadership, character and excellence—girls, just like you, that you will also read about in this book.

In fact, I selected a diverse team of girls and young women of all ages, from all over the country (and even the world) to write this book! Why? Because you deserve to see positive messages, stories and role models!

Just like you heard from my story, when you look for and learn from positive role models, encouraging examples and inspiring stories, they can inspire you and your amazing mind to realize that you can go further, do more, and be more in life than you ever imagined, too!!

What does this mean for you?

Because you can influence who and what you see, this means you can influence who and what you can be!

You know what this means, right? *Imagine I am totally sending you a high five from this page right now!*

Why? Because you are choosing to read this book! You already are a leader inside and you are taking a step to becoming an even bolder one!

Regardless of your past or where you've been, the path to leading an amazing future is paved with the little choices that you make each and every single day.

That's why it's important for you to pay close attention to what you choose to watch, what music you choose to listen to, what you choose to see online, what people you choose to spend time with—and even choices like what you choose to read.

By reading this book, you are making the declaration not to settle for average. By choosing to invest your time and fill your mind with positive messages and read Girls Lead stories, you are becoming part of a movement of amazing girls like you who embrace the message and mission, "Why settle for normal, when you can be extraordinary?!"

Girls Lead is all about making that happen! It's all about "seeing it, to be it!" and painting a bigger vision and better picture of what is possible in your life and how to get there!

As you will see in the following stories of inspiring girls of all ages, you will gain powerful insights on how you can lead your own best life, too—now and in the future!

I want you to know that you are not alone—whatever your struggles or your strengths—every girl—including you—can lead and succeed—and while it isn't always easy, it is worth it!

You will see as you journey through the following pages, that it is definitely true...

Girls *Lead!*

You Lead!

Julie Marie Carrier

P.S. Hey, you leader, you! As you read these words right now, would you be interested in taking one more simple action that your "future you" will want to say thank-you for?

It's easy! Because you care about being your best you, I invite you to join me and other amazing young women leaders at www.BeYOUtifulClub.com

This FREE positive role model, mentoring and leadership club and positive girls' make-a-difference movement is made up of an amazing girls and gals just like you, as well as those who care about helping girls lead lives of character and excellence. We can't do this alone, but together we are unstoppable! After all, girls lead...you lead!

Join the movement and become a part of something awesome by visiting this link:

www.BeYOUtifulClub.com

Run *Your* Best Race!

By
Kylie Nixon

It never really crossed my mind as fun or exciting before—that was before the big tryout.

As a 7th grader, my mom approached me with a proposition.
We were sitting down watching a TV show when it happened.
Her eyes were wide and excited, and a warm smile spread
across her face as she said, "Kylie, there is a cross country
team at your school, and they are holding tryouts in a week.
This may be a great thing for you!"

As she said this, my mind flashed to pictures of my dad
running races—not just any races, we are talking marathons,
triathlons, and even Iron Man competitions! My dad is a
runner who has always loved to run and is really incredible.

I thought about all that went in to preparing for and winning these races plus the fact that I had never really run before. I knew there was no chance that I'd make the cross country team.

My mom, seeing the worry on my face, said, "Kylie, you will love it! Your dad is an amazing runner! Running is in your blood! It's important to try out for new things and interests."

As I reflected on what she said, I was surprised to realize that I had never really had a special interest before—that special something that you love in life that helps you to become your best.

After I realized that I had never really had something to call "my thing," I decided that now was the time to step out and try something new.

I realized that, worst-case scenario, if I tried out and didn't make the team, I'd be no worse off than I had been before. I also thought that in the very unlikely event that I actually made the team and didn't like it, I could always decide not to continue.

As the big tryout got closer, however, I got more and more nervous! At orientation, my insides felt like they were doing flip-flops. As I looked around, I kept thinking that there were so many amazing runners there. Most everyone had already done a season or two. I kept thinking how much better the other runners were than me. I was convinced that I was going to make a fool of myself.

We lined up to do a practice mile jog to warm us up for the official tryout the following day. Even though it was a warm up, I knew the coach was watching, and as we started to jog, I wanted to try to really impress him.

As we started jogging, I fell further and further behind the other runners. The further behind I got, the louder my thoughts were as they shouted, "There is no way that I can do this — I'm so far behind where they are. I can never be the best."

Halfway through, I was literally gasping for air, and every step was a tremendous effort. I kept pushing forward, but it was so hard; I felt like I was going to pass out!

As we neared the end of the practice mile, all the other girls looked like they had barely broken a sweat. It seemed like they didn't even have to try!

As I staggered past the finish line, I was last. I felt totally down.

Shoulders slumped and heavy-hearted, I drifted away from the group toward my mom, who was waiting for me in the car. I thought about how much faster the other girls were — so why should I even try?

My mom said, "How was practice?"

My voice filled with sadness and frustration as I responded, "I don't like running. I don't think it's my thing. I don't want to do this anymore."

My mom said, "Kylie, just tough it out through the week. Even though something may seem really hard at first, it doesn't mean that you shouldn't try."

The truth is that even though all the girls were faster than me, I didn't want to make it look like I quit in the middle of tryouts. That would be even more embarrassing than not making the team!

I sighed, "Okay, Mom, I will try out tomorrow and see how it goes." Secretly, though, I was thinking that if I didn't somehow "love running" by the next day, I wasn't going to do it anymore.

So the day of the big tryout arrived. I was proud of myself that even I went back. I was surprised at my butterflies of excitement that came with allowing myself to hope beyond hope that I would make the team. However, as my thoughts drifted to me being the newest and slowest runner, another part of me was hoping that I wouldn't make the team so I wouldn't have to worry about letting the team down.

The tryouts and running laps were exhausting. I took a silent gasp when the coach announced that we would all have to run another mile. My legs were already so sore from the previous day, and with each lap, they felt like they were turning into lead weights!

As I ran, I was struggling to keep up and was far behind the girls. Comparing myself to the fastest girl, I was in serious doubt that would make the team.

I crossed the finish line. I was so relieved to be finished but embarrassed that I finished last, again.

A glimmer of hope rose, though, as I realized, much to my surprise, that I actually wasn't too far behind the other runners.

After the run the coach had the whole team go to the gym and sit down, he said that he was so impressed with each of us and that we had all done a great job! I was thinking, *What? Me? A good job?*

It turns out...drum roll...that I actually made the cross country team! I couldn't believe it! For the first time in my life, I was actually a part of a team! I felt a mixture of emotions: happiness, fear, excitement, worry!

I made the decision right then and there that even if it was really hard, I was going to run. I was not going to quit.

I was still worried about being the slowest member of the team and letting people down. Something inside me loved the idea of being part of the team more than my fear of letting people down, though.

As practices went on, the first track meet got closer and closer. I couldn't believe that I was going to run in an actual race!

The practices were all really hard, but after practice, I felt really good about myself for having made it through.

Our coach kept saying that the focus is not on being "the fastest" or "the best;" it's about being faster and "your best." It's about pushing yourself to be better than you were yesterday.

This was such a helpful redirect of my focus—and my coach was right! When I was running and I put my focus on comparing myself to the fastest girls who had been doing this for years, I realized that this worry actually made me run slower!

When I was running and, instead, I put my focus on my goal for myself to improve my own running time, I would actually run faster!

With each practice, running was getting easier and easier. Even though I was still not as fast as I wanted to be, I was getting faster. Even so, I was still really nervous about my first track meet running against other schools.

I was a bundle of nerves when the day of the big meet arrived.

Standing there at the starting line, I couldn't believe that I was getting ready to run my first ever race!

They fired the signal to go and I ran! The girls around me took off—and I did, too!

I realized I was actually running my first race! It was thrilling!

That was short lived.

Right before the third mile, nervousness and exhaustion started to creep in. My old habit kicked in, too, and I started comparing myself to the other runners in the lead that were so far ahead of me.

I actually felt like just giving up, stopping, and sitting down.

It was at the moment I wanted to give up that I remembered what my coach had said, "You don't have to be the fastest; run *your* fastest. Don't focus on being 'the best,' focus on being 'your best.' Be better than you were before. Run *your* race."

In that moment, thoughts of comparisons and feelings of hopelessness were replaced with thoughts on running my fastest and being my best. I focused on the finish line. I felt a burst of energy! I felt the wind rush by me as I breathed deeper, pressed harder, and leaped forward. Feelings of joy started to emerge as I began to embrace what running really meant to me.

As I crossed the finish line, I was relieved! My heart felt lighter. I was exhausted but happy. I didn't need to compare myself to others — I didn't have to be "the best" I just had to be *my* best! I had run *my* race — my best race!

Feeling exhilarated, I realized that the most important reward for running doesn't actually come from a trophy — it comes from the inner strength and determination to do your best.

Running your race is just you running against your time. It's not competing against someone else; it's about you continuing to improve.

By focusing on running my best, not only was I a stronger runner but also a stronger person.

It was on the drive home that I was struck by another important realization: I LOVE running! It is "my thing."

I love the action of being able to move myself forward—both physically and mentally. I love the peace that comes with running and it being just me and nature. I value having a dedicated space where I can try harder and push myself to be my best and better than I was before.

Running is an important part of my life now. I get up, and the first thing I do is run. I look forward to practices, too. Even on the days when I don't feel like it, I go to practice anyway, and by the time I'm done, I feel great!

I don't run because I have to or because of awards or medals; I run because I love it and want to continue to push to be my best for next season. My times have also dramatically improved, but no matter how fast I get, I want to keep improving.

Maybe you are not a runner on a track—the truth is, wherever you are right now, you are running your own race in life.

As you run your path in life, comparing yourself to others can distract you from the most important thing: learning, growing, and becoming the best *you* can be.

I'm not saying that you shouldn't try to be number one in something; I'm just saying that real winning means that you improve and better yourself in the process, whether or not you get first place. Far more important than what you get from going after your goal and reaching the finish line is who you become in the process!

The real reward of doing your best is that you run through the twists and turns of life braver, bolder, happier, and more fulfilled — so that in whatever you do, wherever you are, and wherever your path may lead, you run *your* best race!

Don't Become Bitter – Become Better!

By

Marybeth Shields

Drama is not fun. No, I'm not talking about theatre or TV movies. I'm talking about the, "You aren't invited to my party," and, "I am not your best friend today," kind of drama.

At the time it is happening, it hurts and you feel rejected and left out by girls who were your friends yesterday, but not today. When I was in elementary school I experienced this all-too-common girl drama. I think most girls experience this on some level.

As a high-school-age girl, I had thought that I left those drama days behind me. After all, in middle school I had finally established a core group of friends. In fact, most of my middle school and high school experiences were shared with this same group. We went to Friday night football games together; we all went to homecoming as a group; we spent weekends at the beach together, and we hung out as a group on spring break. We also hung out at all of our homes, and as a result, most of our parents became good friends as well. For the most part our group got along well. We stuck up for each other and there was a feeling of security in being part of the group for so long.

Of course, as with many groups, we had one girl in the group, I'll call her Margaret, who I would say was the "Queen Bee" type — the type that if you didn't do what she wanted, you would seriously get stung. She came to power gradually, over time, so I didn't even realize the extent of her influence over us, until much later. Looking back, I see that she was very controlling and even disrespectful to people who were not in our group. She also would get mad at you if you were friendly to people outside our core group of friends (but I didn't care — I was nice to everyone anyway — it's just the way I am.) When she was around, many of us would feel anxious under her judgmental watch and comments. We tended to ignore her criticisms or let her have her way in order to keep the peace — but it wasn't anything I, and our group, couldn't handle. For us, this wasn't drama, it's just the way our group was—and we would all be friends forever.

Like I said, as a rising senior in high school with the same core group of friends for seven years, the drama-filled days of middle school were a distant thing of the past—or so I thought. This all changed in the spring of my senior year when my secure and insulated world came crumbling down around me.

One Friday, I had lunch with Margaret and another friend from my group. We had fun and made plans to hang out that night. I went home and rested and when I got up I texted the two of them to ask what the plans were for the evening. I got a text back. Margaret said, "We have decided not to do anything tonight because there is nothing fun going on." I thought, ok, but that is *weird*. Margaret often had the say in what we were doing, but it wasn't common for us to do nothing. I decided to just hang out at home, watch movies, and catch up on sleep.

I woke up Saturday morning and hopped online to a social networking site out of habit. Much to my surprise and dismay I saw several pictures of all my friends at a party on Friday—including Margaret. My feelings were so hurt. I could not understand why they lied to me.

My mom was out of town and I called her to share how upset I was. She helped me calm down and said there was probably a plausible explanation. She suggested I text them and casually ask what had happened. I tried to be nonchalant and texted them and asked "I thought you guys were not going out last night?" I tried not to sound accusatory even though I was fuming and hurting on the inside.

After several minutes I received a response that was something like: "Well, it was last minute..." This sounded like a lame excuse to me. I live around the corner from one of the girls and five minutes from the other. Neither one offered an apology or any further explanation. I remember sitting in my bedroom feeling hurt, betrayed, and alone. I could not recall anything that I could have said or done to them that would have made them purposely exclude me.

But sadly, it didn't stop there — that weekend marked the beginning of the end of my membership in a core group of close friends that I had been a part of for seven years. Over the course of the next week, Margaret quit calling me and did not return my texts. It didn't stop with Margaret, either. I was slowly excluded from all the group's activities for no apparent reason. I repeatedly made attempts to talk to my friends at school and invite them out — only to have my attempts at conversation and invitations dismissed.

Drama was definitely the operative word here.

I felt so totally alone and devastated. I don't know how to accurately describe the emotional pain I felt, but it was much like the physical pain you have when you are punched in the stomach or you have been hit in the chest and can't breathe. I cycled between feeling bitter, angry, sad, and being in shock. I felt like my world and all my plans were falling down in front of me. I worried, "Who was I going to go with to Spring Break? Who would I hang out with on the Senior Trip? Who was I going to go with to Prom?"

Those unfortunately, were the least of my worries – my whole social life was tied to the friendships in that group. Over the next few weeks, I went through a period of feeling very depressed and lonely. My mom kept encouraging me to reach out to other people and to invite them to go out and do things together. I remember being very aggravated with her. Like me, most people had an established group of friends and it wasn't going to be that easy. I mean who wants to say, "Hi, remember me, I am Marybeth and I know we haven't really been friends the whole four years of high school but let's hang out." In other words, saying it was a lot easier than doing it.

Finally, I had enough! This was my senior year. I realized that my happiness and the outcome of my senior year were in my own hands. I could decide to sit at home and sulk about my situation or to take my mom's advice and reach out to other people at school.

I could choose to become bitter, or become better!

Luckily, unlike Margaret the "Queen Bee," I had not been rude to people that were outside my group and I had always been friendly to others.

Even though I felt self-conscious and wasn't really close to anyone outside my old group, I slowly started reaching out to other people. I was going to make the best of this! I worried that they would think, "Well, now her group has dumped her so she wants to hang with us." Even so, I began inviting others to lunch or to the movies on the weekend.

Guess what? Surprisingly, I found that most people were receptive to my invitations. Before I knew it, I was being invited to hang out with many different people and many different groups.

As I began hanging out with different people, I felt a sense of relief beginning to settle over me. I was puzzled. In part, I felt more comfortable and happier in these new groups. I found that not having the "Queen Bee" around meant that I no longer had to worry about doing and saying the right things. I didn't feel like I had to walk on eggshells and change myself to fit into her rules and expectations. I got to experience, for the first time, what it was really like to be included in a group where all of our ideas and opinions mattered and we accepted each other. I could finally relax and have fun. I felt more freedom than I thought possible.

This made me stop and ask myself: Had I really been that shackled by my relationship with Margaret for all of those years? I had grown up in that group and didn't really understand how fenced in I was, until I experienced what it felt like to be unconditionally accepted by my new friends. I began to wonder how a group of people could ever let one person dictate who they were friends with and how to act.

I am not going to lie, I did miss the close friendships with some of the people in my group and I still struggled with understanding why this had happened – but with my newfound freedom, I decided to leave Margaret's cruelty and my bitterness at the situation behind. I embraced that my life was better off without her.

I made spring break plans with some of the new girls that I had started hanging out with and it was one of the best spring breaks of all my years of high school! Prom time came around and I easily found a new group of friends to go with. We had a blast! The remainder of my senior year went smoothly and I spent a lot of time hanging out with my new friends. I was able to hold my head high, knowing that I had made the best of a tough situation.

When I walked across the stage at graduation, gone was the drama and the stress from my old group. It was replaced by the cheers and smiling faces of my new friends!

In the end, my senior year ended up being better than I could have ever hoped. I had new and better friendships that will last a lifetime — and it didn't stop there!

The lessons I learned about true friendships from that situation allowed me to go to college and meet more amazing new friends who brighten my life so much that my high school drama hurts are just a faint shadow in the past.

I hope that you never have to experience being mistreated by people you believed were your friends, but if you do, you have a choice — *to become bitter* about the situation or *become better* because of it. It is normal to want to hurt those that have hurt you, but this bitterness will get you nowhere. It is up to you to be the *better* person and your *life* will be *better* for it! Please know, as with any tough situation, you have the power to make it through and make not just new friends, but better ones!

I know it can be hard to reach out and make new friends but I encourage you to smile, be genuine, and put yourself out there. Take small steps. Ask people to go to lunch or to join you for a cup of coffee. Think about joining a youth group at church or a service club at school where you will have an opportunity to meet a lot of new people. I think that, like me, you will find that most people will be very receptive to you and your invitations.

My last word of wisdom is that if you find yourself in a "Queen Bee" or drama situation—make sure you don't let her have the throne in your life. Hold your head up high. Choose those friends and groups that you can be yourself with and who value you. Real friends make you feel relaxed and valued, not anxious and judged. If a person does not accept and value you for who you are, do they really deserve your friendship? No, they don't.

Save yourself the drama and don't become bitter—become *better*. You will find better friends and a better life in the process.

Take a Leap Over Fear!

By
Reut Baltinester

It felt like any other day, except, as I sat down in front of my mom so she could help me braid my long, curly red hair, I caught my breath with a sudden realization. My heart began pounding with anxiety and I sat still as a rock, frozen for what felt like forever. As my mother secured the last bobby pin in its place, I allowed myself to think:

"Today is the day of my *first gymnastics competition!*"

It was a long ride to the gymnasium, and it felt even longer because of how nervous I was. Because I had been placed into a higher-level gymnastics team from the start, I didn't get as much practice as the rest of the gymnasts I was going to be competing against. The good news was that I had practiced very hard and felt ready.

We arrived at the competition but my anxiety grew.

The actual competition came so quickly that I didn't even feel like I had time to blink! It was a flurry of activity. I successfully quieted my anxiety by focusing on completing a variety of gymnastics routines including the floor, the bars, and then the balance beam. My worries seemed to melt away! I was feeling on top of the world.

Last but not least, we arrived at the fourth and final event — the vault.

The vault is a special piece of gymnastics equipment with a long upholstered body elevated off the ground that is used for gymnastic moves where you have to jump into the air and handspring over it. (Maybe you've seen one before, it looks a little like the back of a headless horse, and usually is balanced on just one solitary leg instead of four.)

When it was my turn to go, my stomach felt like it was doing flip-flops. As I walked to my starting point, I felt so nervous that my hands and feet began to sweat. I stood there and felt the pressure of everyone's eyes on me. Beads of perspiration began to form on my forehead. As the judges signaled me to go, I wiped my hands and feet and prepared myself.

I looked down the runway at the massive vault and began to run towards it. It felt like the slowest run of my life, when in reality it was really quick. In a blink of an eye, I was hurdling onto the springboard.

As my feet touched the surface of the board, I slipped.

I crashed into the table.

I fell on my face...in front of everyone!

Trying hard to fight back my tears while I shakily stood up, I thought, "I can't believe I messed this up!"

That wasn't the worst part, though. My heart dropped as I realized that I had to go *again* for the second round of the competition!

On the walk back for my second vault, I heard my teammates saying encouraging things like "It's ok," "Second times the charm," and "Just shake it off." None of it worked.

As I prepared for the second vault, I stood unsteadily at the starting point. This time I felt my teammates, coach, judges, and the entire crowd watching me. My mind went blank.

I stepped onto the runway and began running toward the table, only to hurdle myself toward the board and lose my footing! I slipped, crashed into the table and fell on the landing again!

As I stood up from my fall, tears dropped one by one off of my eyelashes and slowly trickled down my cheeks. As I ran back to my team, my tear drops became a flood. I felt humiliated, hurt, and ashamed.

My team hugged me and tried to reassure me that it wasn't as bad as it seemed. I wasn't able to get myself to look on the score board as my very low score flashed up on the screen.

"I totally messed up!" I thought angrily.

The day went by slowly as I waited for my teammates to finish competing so I could escape the gym. When the competition was over and I found my mom, she saw how hurt I was, and hugged me like only a mom can. I was in no mood to talk. Anxiety gripped my heart as I thought, "There is no way that I can ever do the vault again."

Sparked by those traumatic falls, I grew terrified of vaulting. I wasn't able to get myself to do it. Every practice I would go to vault but, every time, fear would get the better of me and I would end up running off to the side of the table. There were times when my coach would make me try to vault almost the entire practice. I would get incredibly frustrated because my fear kept telling me I couldn't do it. Over time my coach lost hope in my vaulting abilities and so did I. Almost half a year passed by without me vaulting at all.

Then I moved to a different gym. At my new gym my coach helped me learn that you can never let your fear get the best of you. You have to believe in yourself more than your fear. She helped me get back up on that vault!

She wouldn't give up on me, no matter how difficult it was. Instead of facing my huge fear of the vault all at once, my new coach helped me take little steps. At first we did simple drills to work on my run and my jump. From there we started vaulting on low and squishy mats. After success with that, we went on the actual table, but with a protective mat both behind the vault and on top of it. I was making clear progress, though it was still pretty difficult and sometimes I would cry out of frustration. Still, my coach wouldn't give up on me, and through her words of encouragement, she helped me make sure that I didn't give up on myself.

Once I was able to master each small step and overcome my fear little by little, we would go to the next level. She stood right by the vault and helped me over every time, giving me that extra confidence I needed to face my fear once and for all.

After I became a master doing the vault with a protective mat on the floor and my coach's help by my side, came the real challenge! It was time for me to attempt the vault with no coach! My coach said, "You're not leaving here until you vault, alone!"

This time it was only me and the vault. My fear crept back up and started picking at me with negative thoughts, "You can't do this. Just quit!" But, at that moment, I remembered what my coach had taught me. I decided to believe in myself more than my fear!

"Stop it!" I told the growing voice of fear. I said to myself in a much louder voice of inner encouragement, "You can do this. You have practiced. You are ready. Just go for it!" I went for it!

I felt my feet hit the landing as I had successfully completed the vault on my own. My heart burst with excitement. Victory!

I had completed what I had worked so hard to achieve. At that moment, I felt proud. I was proud of all the work I had put into overcoming my fear and the outcome. By taking small steps with my coach to overcome my worry, believing in myself more than my fear became easier. I was able to reach my goal of doing the vault again!

It didn't stop there. All of the extra practice paid off and *the vault actually became one of my best events!*

Wow! The voice of my fear about the vault was extinguished forever — or so I thought.

I learned that my next competition was coming up and it happened to be in the *exact same gym* where the terrible vault occurred about a year ago.

Even with so many successes behind me as one of the top vaulters on my team, when I arrived at the competition, my stomach tightened as the image of my fall replayed in my head again and again.

I prepared for my warm ups before the competition and had to stand in the exact same spot as I had before my fall. All of the terrible memories and feelings from that day came back in full force! My fear screamed through my mind, saying "You are going to totally mess up. You are going to fall!"

I ran towards the vault in my practice run and, when I reached the springboard, I stopped. My fear paralyzed me and I was not able to leap over the vault!

Then it was time to compete. Anxiety and fear continued to consume my thoughts, "Give up! You are gong to mess this up." I stopped everything and took a deep breath. I decided to face my fear, straight on.

Instead of believing my fear that told me the reasons why I was not going to succeed, I took a moment to believe in the reasons *why I was going to succeed!*

I focused on how much I had prepared for this moment. I thought about my amazing vaults in practice and other competitions. I thought about how much I had grown stronger through facing my fears before. Funny enough, the more I believed in myself, the quieter my voice of fear became. It wasn't even an audible whisper when I kept saying, "I can do this. Just go for it!"

As I prepared for my turn, I put tons of chalk on my hands and feet to soak up my remaining nervous sweat. As I saluted the judges I took a deep breath and told myself again, "I can do this. Just go for it!"

By choosing to believe in myself, I took a leap over my fear! I jumped over the same vault that had crushed my confidence almost a year ago, and now my confidence levels soared above it!

Not only did I do the vault, but I did it very well. I won first place!!!!

Most importantly I rose above my fear of the vault and parted with it forever!

While I was happy to have done so well, I realized that more important than any medal was the lesson I learned. I learned that no matter what roadblock or fear I am facing, I can make it through by believing in myself more than in my fear.

The same is true for you, too! You may encounter obstacles, fears, tough times, problems or challenges on your journey of life, but you need to know that you will be able to overcome them.

You are an incredibly strong, smart, and beautiful person. You have talents and gifts for a purpose.

When you try to reach a big goal or realize your dreams, it will not always be easy—and sometimes fear will try to block your path.

What do you do?

Believe in yourself, face your fear head on and *leap over it!*

Dress Up with True Beauty!

By
Rachel Thor

Abby looked sadly at her New Year's Eve party dress she had brought for later in the week. She is a thin, fair-skinned blonde with soft cheeks and big eyes, and I could see that the dress was just too big for her delicate frame.

"I think I'll try to sew it to make it fit," she said.

"The front desk usually has free mini sewing kits for guests," I told her. (I knew this because it seemed that every time my family of six went on a vacation, somebody tore something, and my mom always asked the hotel staff if they had any.) There would hopefully be enough breaks at our conference for her to fix it before the party. I secretly worried that the little sewing kit wasn't going to be able to do enough to help, though.

We took the elevator down from our tenth floor room to the lobby. I had no problem going with her for such a simple task. What an easy way to give! Besides, my dress for the party later that week was already perfect, and I couldn't wait for us to look stunning at the dance.

My dress was fantastic! Both quirky and elegant, the top was knit with white lacey designs and purple-brown trim. The skirt of the dress floated away in a mist of white fabric with a gorgeous silk slip underneath. Depending on the way the light hit, the dress could look white, black, and silver all at once! It felt heavenly, and I'd found it when I was traveling in Belgium during one of the best travel abroad weekends of my life. This dress, to me, symbolized everything I was on the inside, or wanted to be: beautiful, meaningful, and radiant. (Even though it was a little small around the top, I knew I could make it work with a camisole underneath, and it would still look great). I had been holding onto this dress dearly for six months since I found it in Belgium, waiting for the perfect occasion to wear it! Finally, at this exciting event with hundreds of friends and strangers alike, I would get to put it on and would show the world who I was in my perfect dress!

The conference flew by, and the time of the New Year's Eve party had finally arrived. It was going to start in less than thirty minutes, and we rushed back to our room to change! It was such a busy and incredible week with very little down time!

"Ah! I forgot to sew it!" Abby frowned as she tried on her dress. She was swimming in the black cotton top, even with the thick elastic waistband to pull it in. The grey ruffled skirt that swallowed her didn't help the cause either. Something needed to be done, quickly.

I thought to myself about the possible options:

Sew the dress? Nope. We were out of time, and I haven't sewn anything in a while!

What about safety pin it from the inside? Yeah, that would work! We have all those pins in the sewing kit! Oh no, I remember Abby told me they had all been used to hold together the remnants of her shoes. That wouldn't work either.

Suddenly a third idea popped into my head and out of my mouth so quickly that I didn't have time to analyze what I was doing. I blurted out, "Want to switch dresses?"

I thought, *Did I just say that?!* I felt my heart drop. I held my breath as I realized the implications. I had just pitted my self-focused will to wear my own gorgeous dress against my moral compass that told me a girl's happiness is worth so much more than a piece of clothing for a silly dance.

"Are you sure that's alright?" she asked me, worried.

"Yeah, definitely. It's not a big deal," I said as I forced a smile. I was still trying to fully convince myself of this as I reluctantly handed over my incredible dress.

Abby tried on my dress and looked AMAZING! The top that had been too small for me fit her tiny frame perfectly. The purple shoes she had brought along matched my dress better than my own shoes! Seeing how oddly perfect everything about the dress seemed to work for her, I knew that it was meant to be. I hoped I would be as lucky when I tried her dress on.

I was not. Don't get me wrong; it was a very cute dress, but it seemed to point out every insecurity I had about my body. The short center of the dress made me feel like my torso was shrinking. The grey frills seemed to balloon around my already curvy hips until I felt like an ostrich. I tried to focus on a positive note—at least my black shoes matched this dress to a tee.

As I looked at my reflection while wearing Abby's dress, for a moment I desperately wanted to take my dress back! I wanted to wear my dress again because I thought the dress would make me beautiful instead of how dumpy I felt in this ugly grey dress.

As I looked at how happy Abby was, though, my begrudging heart started to change. She was positively radiant! She looked gorgeous! Her eyes were bright, and her smile sparkled! She was beautiful.

But her happiness soon became clouded with another emotion. Knowing Abby, I saw that she started to feel a little guilty with my gesture of kindness and friendship. It dimmed her features and kept her from shining like she had been moments before. I knew that as she wore my dress, her guilt would make her feel the need to explain that it wasn't really her dress but mine each time she got a compliment, and this weight would keep her from enjoying the party.

I thought to myself, What is a gift worth if it comes with an extra dose of guilt, as if she owes me something? Then it's really not a gift at all.

I knew what I had to do, so I told her, "I really don't want to have to explain the dress switch thing all night. Let's not tell anybody and just have a rockin' New Year in our awesome dresses!" I watched that guilty weight lift from her shoulders as gratitude and joy poured back into her eyes. There were no strings attached, for either of us. Seeing her joy at my gift — joy and happiness started to fill up my heart, too.

We finished getting ready and were beaming with smiles and laughter as we strutted through the hotel halls together, truly enjoying the evening.

People stopped us time and again and told us both how beautiful we looked.

Soon we'd forgotten all about what we were wearing as we rocked out on the dance floor. At the stroke of midnight, as all 900 students cheered and celebrated the start of the new year — I celebrated something else, too.

We were having so much fun! We were enjoying celebrating together as friends! We smiled and laughed until our cheeks hurt!

Seeing Abby's joy and my own, I realized something else, too.

We *both* felt beautiful!

Even with Abby wearing my shimmery dress and me wearing her awkward grey one, I realized that feeling truly beautiful actually has a lot less to do with what you wear on the *outside* and a lot more to do with what you choose to wear on the *inside*.

As I saw how happy Abby was with my gift, the dress that I'd hoped would make me feel beautiful on my own paled in comparison to how beautiful and alive I felt when I "put on" a spirit of generosity and helped my friend.

The same is true for you!

Your beauty shines from the inside out as you radiate qualities like joy, happiness, gratitude, and kindness! These inner qualities outshine even the most beautiful outfit, accessory, or pair of designer shoes — or dress from Belgium, for that matter!

Your beauty radiates from the smile you bring to a friend and the joy this brings to your heart.

Your beauty shines brighter as you say a kind word and use your strengths and gifts to help others!

Your beauty glows as you encourage someone going through a tough situation or lend a helping hand.

Your beauty sparkles even more as you take a few moments to feel grateful for the good things in your life or say thank you to someone who cares about you.

Each day, you get to choose what to wear, and far more powerful than any specific clothing choice are those beautiful inner qualities and gifts that you choose to show the world.

So, each morning as you think about what you are going to choose to wear, remember to choose wisely — put on your best qualities and dress up with true beauty!

Dare to Be
Different – BE YOU!

By
Ellie Smith

"Different."

The dictionary defines <u>different</u> as "partly or totally unlike in nature, form or quality."

Actually, that sounds pretty good to me – especially the part about "partly unlike in nature or quality." At the same time, I have to admit that being "different" did cause me some difficulty (OK, a LOT of difficulty) for a few years.

I actually like to be "different." To be different is to quietly celebrate how I am unique among the billion of other people on this Earth! I am the one and only me! You, too! That is to say, you are the one and only you! You are just like me — in that you're totally different from everyone else! Pretty cool, huh?

It's good — that's the way it's supposed to be! That's what makes life interesting!

I have to admit, it wasn't always easy to dare to be different. At first it was pretty easy. Looking back, I was different from the start. It was great and all, but what kind of baby tries to "sing/coo/babble" to Christmas carols before he or she can even walk, or talk, for that matter? I mean, that's a little freaky, right? And while I don't remember it at all (hey, I was 3 months old!), my mom swears it actually happened, and I've come to believe she's pretty much always right.

OK, so I showed a little musical interest at an unusually early age. That seemed to work out pretty well in my early kiddie music, march-around-the-room, beat-on-a-drum, sing-song classes. At the ripe old age of 3, during a particularly large family reunion, as the band took a well-earned break, I somehow found my way onto the stage, and, tip-toeing toward a too-tall microphone, I proceeded to serenade the crowd with multiple repetitions of the same song, over, and over, and over, and over!

All this carried me right into Pre-K, as well, where I spontaneously announced on the very first day of class to the teacher and all the students that, "I would like to sing a song!" A very patient and loving teacher was kind enough to oblige, and I alone, soloed at the top of my lungs, what I'm sure was a really swell rendition (OK, maybe not!!) of a song from a popular musical! (I should note that my memory is that no one else sang that day, or even asked to! Can you imagine that?!? He he!)

Different is definitely the operative term here! "Ellie loves to sing" seemed to be an acceptable explanation for all this up until about the middle of my fourth grade year.

Something awful happened at about the age of 10-11. Everything seemed to be changing as we started to grow up—but some chose to handle changes in not-so-good ways! Change can be a scary word that threatens our fun and our freedom just to be kids. It's no one's fault, and it's not really all that awful because change is necessary in all of our lives. It's just that some tend to act differently as they change, and it probably feels a lot safer for some if they act tough, or cool, and above all, if they don't stand out—which really means, try not to be different, blend in!

So it seemed at this point in middle school everyone's "uniqueness" had somehow become "unacceptable behavior," at least to the kids who were quickly moving from "fun" to "frigid." It soon became painfully obvious that a kid like me who loved to sing had become unacceptably different from these emerging models of the adolescent 'in-crowd.'

No, my grades hadn't suddenly dropped, my appearance was pretty much the same as it had always been (or just a bit more awkward), and we all still wore exactly the same school uniforms, but we were growing up. The girls who continued to bear a striking resemblance to what once had been my closest unique friends, seemed now to have become possessed by aliens from the planet "COOL." Their uniqueness was replaced by cookie-cutter styles, conversation topics, and interests. In the effort to "fit in" they lost themselves — and that was really hard for me because, change or not, I am different. I am me!

I would love to tell you that I just ignored the teasing and the cruelty from groups of kids who used to be my best friends. When it began, I thought that it might go away if I tried to become a part of the "in-crowd." Try as I might, they thought that I just wasn't "cool enough." I've always been a singer, performer, and probably a bit of a "theater nerd," but a good production of the hit musical, "Les Miserables" just wasn't what my old friends enjoyed. The harder I tried to fit in, the harder it became.

From late in my fourth grade year, all the way through middle school, the meanness continued, and even intensified. I was constantly teased, ridiculed and rejected; with their objective being to humiliate and emotionally hurt me. The payoff for them was usually a laugh at my expense, or worse, making me cry. Unfortunately, it was often effective, and went on far too long! There were many days when I would get into my mom's car after school, and just cry. I constantly wondered what was wrong with me that made me the target of teasing, rejection, and cruelty.

Even though it was difficult, rather than try to blend in under the pressure, I decided to continue to embrace my differences more than ever! I never lost my love for my passion, or my passion for my love — singing, acting, and performing. In fact, it probably only intensified during those years that I was bullied. Performance was my outlet, my expression of myself. It seems that every weekend, I was singing the National Anthem at a baseball, basketball, or football game in front of thousands of people. If I wasn't at Dodger Stadium, I may have been at a Mavs game in Dallas, or singing for the Bears in Chicago, maybe even the Mets in New York; or contributing my voice and talent at an event for charity, helping to raise millions of dollars over the years for people in need. I loved every moment of it and knew that no amount of teasing would ever get in the way of being different.

Late in my eighth grade year, because I could no longer contain the hurt, pain, and teasing from the other students, I finally decided that enough was enough, and I began to speak out! This was absolutely my best decision EVER! I began to pour out the events of the past years to my family and to those who really loved me.

When I began to open up and talk about what was going on, I finally understood. I was simply being BULLIED! As I shared my story, I began not only to feel better, but to gain a new sense of myself, my uniqueness and how important I am — as we all are! I began to realize that the problem was never with me, but with the bullies themselves. As I began to share my own story, I also found that what I experienced was in no way unique to my school, or to any other, for that matter. I knew that I needed to do something to help stand up for other students who were being bullied too.

Buoyed by the confidence of sharing my story and the passion I had for music, by the time I was 13 I had begun to work with a music team in L.A. while also writing and recording some original music. One of the original songs that we generated was a song called "Don't Let It Get to You." The lyrics seemed to come together naturally, about people who have had a hard time, who need to pick themselves up, and get beyond the negative experience. The words in the verse seemed to come from within:

"It's gettin' over here, it's gettin' over there, it's gettin' everywhere; Don't-let-it-get-to-you!"

We recorded the song and it was such a success, I found myself talking to a music video director about my years of being bullied. It was through this conversation that the vision came together for my first music video, a video that could be used to reach millions of kids to raise awareness about bullying!

Over the next several weeks/months, we shot a music video that is a story about social bullying, set in a school classroom, all built upon my original song, "Don't Let It Get to You."

We immediately began getting a lot of positive feedback.

Still, I knew that there was something more, something very important, that had to be done.

I knew I had to share my story with kids who might be experiencing the same situation that I had during my earlier years in order to reach even more kids. So just before the beginning of my sophomore year in high school, together with my mom and dad, and armed with my music video, we put together "my story," my music video and my message, to share with every student I could possibly reach in my community, my state, and, eventually, across the country.

Honing my message to a half-hour presentation starting with my 3-minute video, we met first with our community's school board, who set up meetings with the key administration people in our huge school district—the fifth largest in the nation—so we could share my story and offer to deliver it in schools to help stop bullying. In short, they loved my story. It was "real" because it was true. Plus, it would be delivered by a young person, to younger kids, and it all began with the 'language' that kids love most—a pop music video!!

Most important, it was a story about bullying, self-worth, self-confidence, and self-esteem. It was an interactive presentation where I talked about the value and importance of every person in the room. I affirmed that we are all unique, special and, yes, different and the students learned that people with a good sense of self-esteem DO NOT BULLY. We end the half hour session with a rousing song and dance to that verse from my song:

"It's gettin' over here; it's gettin' over there; it's gettin' everywhere. Don't-let-it-get-to-you!"

I have now presented my anti-bullying message "Bullying: Don't Let It Get to You" at nearly 100 schools and to more than 40,000 students. My "payback" comes in the form of reading all the notes, posts, and comments from the kids, including over 25,000+ online comments from students on my videos, alone. And the best rewards of all come from the hugs, laughter and joy—especially the look in other kids' eyes as they realize the beauty and perfection in discovering and celebrating that we are all, well—different!!

In my 17 years of life, I have been blessed, yes, with a talent for singing and performing, but I have been especially blessed through the lessons that I learned as a result of my years of being bullied.

That's right...I said "BLESSED!" My real life experiences are joined together with my musical talents in order to reach out to kids everywhere who are bullied, threatened, or maybe feel "less than" because they fear they might be different from others. And I get to help thousands of kids to maybe begin to feel a little better about themselves.

The blessings that come from giving to others continue to pour into my life. In order to further my message about bullying awareness, I decided to enter a local pageant, a first-ever event for me. To my great surprise, I won! From there, I went on to compete in the state pageant. Using my voice as my talent, and my anti-bullying campaign as my platform, I won the state pageant and the state title! There are 4 elements to my title: scholarship, style, success and, most important of all, service. Each of these is represented by the four points of the crown that I was able to wear. I was also grateful to receive the Youth in Philanthropy Award and the Young Hero of the Year Award in recognition of my impact helping so many students!

Wow! All of this because, through it all, I dared to be *different!*

Maybe you are being bullied or maybe you have been in the past or will be in the future. How do you know if you are being bullied? As I share in my presentations to students as a speaker, when most people think about bullying, they probably think about a big burly kid at school threatening a much smaller one, possibly a physical attack intended to relieve the victim of his lunch money, and, oh, by the way, of his dignity, too! Actually, I want you to remember the fact is that most bullying is not physical–it is emotional.

Social bullying is often done repeatedly, not only to isolate or exclude someone, but to intimidate them and to make them feel sad and hurt. Even if someone is not bullying you to your face, you can be the victim of bullying in other ways, too. Today, social media has also become a center for a special type of bullying: cyber-bullying. That is particularly cruel, because many kids, thinking that they are anonymous, will write words online that they would otherwise never actually say in real life!

Regardless of the type of bullying that you may face, if you are ever in a bullying situation, remember to tell someone right away.

Also, if you are being bullied, I want you to remember the "problem" is not with you, but with the bullies themselves. Bullies are never driven to bully because they are strong and confident. They bully because they are really weak in character and lacking in confidence. I never met a bully with a healthy sense of self-esteem. And those who share those weaknesses tend to band together with others because they don't have the "strength to be strong," they don't have the "confidence to be confident," and they don't have the self-esteem to stand-up for themselves.

It's amazing how far I've come since that difficult time that started in 4th grade. While I can't go back and talk to myself when I was going through those difficult times — I can share with you that your life can turn out amazing when you embrace your differences and rise above the bullying.

When you go though bullying — you can choose to blend in or embrace your differences!

Choose to embrace your differences! Don't let it get to you! Dare to be different — BE YOU!

Carpe Diem!

— *By* —
Chloe Diamond

I was born in Yi-Yang city, Hunan Province, China. It was so hot there that my parents were ready to leave as soon as they came to get me. Against all odds with twelve other infants, I was somehow the one chosen — the lucky one in the orphanage that day.

Rather than be a forgotten and lonely child in an awful situation, I was adopted and was going to America! My family knew I would get along with them because when I first saw my dad, I clung onto his leg for several minutes, never leaving his side. Together with my sister, Nicole, we thankfully have both come a long way from our orphanage in China.

My parents said that when I first came to America when I was a year and two months old, I spoke to them in Chinese. Thankfully, I quickly learned how to speak English.

In elementary school, when I was old enough to begin to understand my unique start in life, my parents told me that I was adopted from China. I was not really upset or worried because I knew in my heart that even if I was born in China, my parents and my sister here in the U.S. are my family. I knew that they loved me and that they gave me a better life and better opportunities than I would have had otherwise. They gave me my best chance.

As a young girl growing up, thoughts about my humble beginnings began to fade into the background, as I enjoyed a roof over my head, a hot meal every night, buying books, reading, golfing, being able to play in my backyard and calling my friends to hang out. These were such a normal part of my life that I began to take them for granted and think that I lived in my own little world that revolved mostly around me. But that started to change as I got older. As I began to further embrace my story and where I came from, I learned more about that poverty-stricken orphanage in Yi-Yang City, Hunan Province, China.

My mom is one of the biggest influences in my life. She helped me understand about gratitude. She helped me learn how there are so many kids around the world that don't have the same privileges that I have now. Some people don't have access to running water or food. Millions of young people don't even have the opportunity to go to school or read books. So many other kids are forced to work at a young age because they don't have anywhere else to go. Other kids don't even have a place to call home. I realized this *easily* could have been me!

As I entered 7th grade with my eyes much more aware of what was going on in the world, I made a choice that rather than take things for granted, I would try to be grateful for what I have. Rather than let life just happen, I would go out and live life's opportunities to the fullest! I would decide to *carpe diem* — a Latin phrase that means "seize the day!"

When it came to how I spent my time each day, I decided that rather than sitting inside staring at my phone and thinking "I'm bored," I would instead carpe diem! I would seize the day by going outside to enjoy the beautiful weather and have fun!

Rather than arguing about the dinner my mom made or complaining about how I didn't want to eat the vegetables, I would instead try to be grateful that I had food to eat and would think about how fortunate I am to actually have a healthy meal. In some countries, they live on just rice and beans or just the food they are able to grow in a little patch of dirt outside their shack that they call home.

Rather than complaining about how I have too much homework and how I wish the school year were over, I would redirect my thoughts to how I need to be grateful for the fact that I even get to go to school and learn. While education and school is a normal thing for students in some countries, in many countries it is a privilege that is not offered to all young people. Even having a book may be considered a luxury.

When it comes to my sports practice, rather than thinking, "Uh, I don't really feel like going—I'd rather just sit here and surf the Internet or watch this show," I would pause and carpe diem! I would seize the day by getting up and thinking about how fortunate I am to have this opportunity to become better, develop discipline, grow from pushing myself to be my best, and extend the limits of what I think I can do. In some countries, young people don't even have the choice to play a sport or do an afterschool activity—they are instead forced to work in factories where they don't even know what it's like to follow their dreams or reach for their own goals.

While it's not always easy, I try to remind myself to be grateful and seize the day, every day!

Carpe diem isn't just a phrase—it's a wise saying to live by.

I also don't try to take it too far, either. What is too far? Too far is what a lot of negative media portrays as "living life" to girls and teens. It often shows ridiculous images that tell us that "living in the moment" is getting drunk, doing drugs, or doing things that are not smart for someone's future. These things can have big consequences that can actually block you from living life to the fullest. Unhealthy or destructive choices are the opposite of carpe diem. I believe that seizing the day means that you do things that will ultimately *help you* become better, make your future brighter, and *help others* around you—whether you help your friends, family, or community.

Your first step to living a life where you carpe diem doesn't mean that you need to try to change the whole world either—you can start with yourself first and branch out to help your community and your school.

As you begin your day, you can start making the most of your life by being actively grateful or taking another seemingly small action that will keep you on track.

Sometimes the simplest decision can make even the unhappiest day a better one. As with any habit or situation you want to change to more effectively seize the day, you can start small. It may be as easy as taking a brief technology break for a few minutes.

For example, I use my phone just as much the next person, but making the choice to put it down for a short time to read a real book, play a game outside, or just have a good time connecting with friends in person can really change your outlook on the world that day. As the minutes add up into hours, you will find that as you unplug more from your screen, you will plug in more to what matters most in life—real-life laughter, in-person smiles, and more meaningful connections with your family and friends.

As you do the little things that help to make the best of every day, those days turn into weeks and those weeks into months—and those little things turn into big things! Before you know it, you will be living more in the moment and will be present with your family, friends, and community. You will feel more grateful, happier, and can be even more successful, too.

Live each day to the fullest and seize the day! The *present* is a present—carpe diem!

Never Give Up!

——————— *By* ———————
Jenna Phelps

The call came at 9:15 a.m. on August 25 over ten years ago. Within minutes after answering the phone, my mom arrived at my school and removed me from my fourth grade classroom. An hour later, we boarded the private plane that had been waiting for us at our local airport. It was a beautiful day to fly — and a beautiful day to begin my new life.

My mom and I talked during the entire flight to the Houston Medical Center in Houston, Texas, mostly about what would happen that day. I had no idea, at the time, how concerned my mom was. She hid it from me very well so that I wouldn't be nervous.

When we landed in Houston, we were met by an ambulance and a crew called "The Kangaroo Crew." We were immediately taken to the huge medical center, the largest pediatric hospital in the United States at the time. To me, the ride seemed endless. I couldn't see where we were going, and I didn't know much about what was going to happen. One thing I knew for certain: my mom would have taken my place in an instant, if she could.

Once I was admitted into the hospital, at least 20 people gathered around my bed. They took my blood pressure, collected blood samples, and inserted an IV into my arm. Everyone was in a rush to meet the preparation deadline.

Meanwhile, my mom had to sign countless forms. Even though I had been in the hospital many, many times in my life, I didn't fully understand what was happening on this day, but I knew it was the day where I would be getting a liver transplant! Even though I was scared and a lot could go wrong, I made a choice: never give up!

After all the tests indicated that my body could undergo the operation, I was rushed into surgery. I said goodbye to my mom, who had put on a brave face for me. This wasn't the first time she watched as I was rolled away for medical treatment. At the age of just 2 1/2, I was diagnosed with leukemia, a cancer of the white blood cells, and underwent chemotherapy for the next 2 1/2 years. I had numerous spinal taps and surgeries during that time. At the age of eight, I started having seizures that couldn't be controlled by medicine...and now this. But I had to remind myself, no matter what I'd been through or have to go through ahead, "Never give up!"

Within hours, my dad and grandparents had arrived and joined my mom during the tense wait. Everyone had been rushing from different cities to reach the hospital before I came out of surgery. My Grandma Banny even brought my pet fish.

After five hours of surgery, my doctor went to my family with the news. The transplantation was a success: I had a new liver!

I spent the first night in the hospital intensive care unit (ICU), connected to a number of machines. I came in and out of consciousness, mostly remembering that I was in tight hose to prevent any blood clots in my legs. After 30 hours in the ICU, I went to the transplant floor and began taking 32 pills a day. The transplant suture ran 12 inches down the middle of my chest and 15 inches across my stomach, and was held together by 53 staples. My scar looks like a peace sign without the circle around it. It is my badge of courage; it shows me I am a survivor! Even with all the tubes, surgeries, and scary times, I never gave up!

On my first day out of the ICU, I had to get up and walk. I didn't feel like it because I was so sore, but I remembered that I never give up! So I got up!

It felt good to get out of bed. It was difficult to sit in a chair, and even harder to get up from it. The nurses kept telling me how much better I would feel, the more I walked. I did laps around the hospital floor with my IVs and the IV pole, and was proud when I accomplished my daily lap goal. Although I never earned a medal for speed, I gave myself a big "E" for effort. Throughout my ordeal, the doctors, nurses, transplant group and my child-life coordinator were absolutely wonderful. I felt so grateful to the person who had donated their liver to me — they literally gave me life!

Before I returned home, I had a feeding tube inserted through my nose and into my stomach. This was no fun. When not in use it would hang out of my nose about 24 inches onto my chest. I wouldn't let anyone take pictures of me with that awful tube in my nose. A home health nurse came to the house and showed my mom how to feed me a nutrient-rich chocolate drink through the tube at night. It would be years before I could look at chocolate milk in the same way. Despite the tube feedings several times every night and trying to eat regular food throughout the day, I lost 30 pounds. My weight dropped to 73 pounds, which was dangerously low for my height. Even though I knew something was wrong and had many down days, I kept on! Why? Because I never give up!

After a few weeks, the feeding tube clogged, so we headed to the emergency room. My mom asked the doctor, "Who can eat with that thing down their throat? If you take that out of her nose, she'll eat!" Sure enough, the doctor removed the tube, and I started to eat a lot! I craved tacos. Breakfast, lunch, and dinner, I couldn't get enough of them. I began to gain weight almost immediately.

After the first year of my transplant, my life was back on track until the summer of my 18th Birthday. I spent almost my entire summer vacation in the hospital and turned eighteen in a hospital bed. My face was puffy from all the steroids that were helping to treat the organ rejection and it took months for the swelling to go down. I had numerous complications. I will be honest; there were tough days when I didn't feel like keeping on. There were days that I didn't know if I was going to make it. It was on this type of day, though, when I would dig my heels in and say "Never give up!" and, what do you know, eventually, things did start to get better! Though it was the hardest thing I've done in my life, I pushed through.

I learned, as it turns out, even though tough times *feel* like they will last forever— when you keep on keeping on, you learn those challenges actually are temporary and better days are ahead. How do I know? I went on to do things I never dreamed would be possible!

I went on to become a cheerleader in my high school, an Ambassador for a international positive role model and mentoring club for girls, the BeYOUtiful Club®, wrote my own book "Get Up!" and launched a national speaking career where I inspire other people who are going through tough times and challenges. I feel very blessed to be able to do all of these wonderful things, now! Thankfully, I never gave up!

No, life isn't always perfect. It never is. I may not have as much energy as the other people that are healthy, but that doesn't stop me from doing what I can.

I've learned a lot from all of these challenges. I don't let the small things in life get me down. If I have a problem, I ask myself, "Is this life threatening?" If not, then it's much less of a problem than it could be. It has also made me stronger in my faith. I know I am here for a special purpose — just like you and everyone! It has also taught me to keep going no matter what and that better days are ahead. Keep pushing through and, believe me, your future you will want to thank you for it!

Just as I've learned to overcome setbacks and go on to do amazing things that I never thought I could, you can too! You have more strength and courage within you than you can imagine! You can get through even the most difficult challenges and go on to live a wonderful life. I'm living proof!

No matter what happens, no matter how difficult the challenge, or how overwhelming the situation in life may feel, you can push through to a better and brighter life than you ever thought possible!

How?

Never give up!

Turn Those Tough Times Around

— By —

Nais Acevedo

"Are you sure she can't hear us?" said my mom. "Do you want someone to take her into another room while we talk?" the court appointed advisor responded.

"Yes, please," said my mom.

She looked at me from across the room with worried eyes. I could tell that she was hoping that I didn't hear what she just said about the divorce, my dad and what they were fighting about. She knew it would make me sad—and she was right.

The advisor had me moved into another room. I stared out the window wondering what would happen. It was a dismal, cloudy day. My parents were young when they got married and it didn't work out. I remember all the stress that was going on in our family. They all tried to act like everything was ok but I knew it wasn't. And now this – a court battle over where I would live.

(It was complicated. My mom eventually got remarried to a wonderful man named Keefe. His job required him to move to Texas and this meant my mom wanted to move with me, too. My dad didn't want me to move – and then began the battle over where I'd live.)

The verdict came in and the court decided that I would live in Texas with my mom during the school year and I'd live with my dad in Arizona during the summer.

At first, it was really hard leaving my family in Arizona. The toughest part was going to the airport. My dad never cries but he got teary-eyed when he had to drop me off the first couple of times at the airport. At first, every flight was hard. I would look at whoever was taking me to the plane and I would start crying.

The whole situation made me really sad. I didn't like being sad, I mean, who does? I tried to shake it off, but at first I couldn't. My mind went back to the question I constantly asked myself, "Why couldn't my mom and dad just have stayed together?" To make it even more challenging, when I was staying with my mom and family in Texas, I kept thinking about how much I missed my dad and my family in Arizona. When I was staying with my dad and my family in Arizona over the summer, I kept thinking about how much I missed my mom and my family in Texas. I also thought about how much I missed all my friends doing things together over the summer without me.

I was sad no matter where I was—and I realized that this way of thinking clearly was not working. I realized that I needed to stop focusing on all the negative things that were going on because when I focused on those things, it just made me feel worse. So instead of focusing on the past, I started to focus more on the present. During the summer when I was in Arizona, instead of focusing on how I was not with my mom and family in Texas, I focused on how happy my dad was to see me. When I missed my friends in Texas, I focused on how my family spoiled me big time when I was in Arizona and how I felt like a little queen. I have to admit, I loved it!

Also, when I would start feeling sad about the divorce, I would remind myself that the divorce was not my fault and even though my parents did get a divorce, I got my step dad and my siblings—even more people to love and more people who love me! As I did this, over time, I started feeling much better about myself and the situation, but I didn't stop there!

I began to realize that while I couldn't control the situation, I could choose how to respond. There were even more ways that I could influence how I felt! If you are in a similar situation or going through a tough or challenging time, you can try to do some of these things, too. Here are four things I did to help myself feel better:

1. **Stay Active!**

   When I was sad, I found that it really helps to be active in a positive way! I feel better when I dance, run, play football, basketball, or baseball. My favorite sport is soccer. I can get all my stress out by running and kicking the ball.

   On one particular day when I was feeling really sad, I knew that I didn't feel like working out, but I asked myself, "Do I want to keep doing the same thing and feel down, or do I want to do something different to be happy?" I decided to stay active to get happy. It wasn't an immediate response, but over time I started to feel happy and stronger!

   To get active, you can try to do something athletic. If that doesn't work out for you, you can do things like reading, drawing or even just playing interactive computer games. If you are doing something you love, then you won't be obsessing about the tough or difficult time you went through. Also, you can go out and do something once in a while like going shopping or to the movies. *What are some positive things that you can do to stay active?*

2. Talk About It!

Rather than keeping my feelings to myself, I began to talk about them more and this helped too! My friends really helped me get through the tough times. I could call or text them anytime. They gave me hugs and said things were going to be okay. We also had sleepovers and went to the mall. If you have step-parents, even if you don't have a strong connection with them at first, you can still talk to them. Be nice and it can make you happier. I talked to my grandparents, too. It helped me a lot and made me feel better.

It's OK to talk with other people about how you feel and the tough situation you are in, whether it's a professional like a counselor or your mom, your dad, a step-parent, grandparents, friends or someone else you trust. Some good advice and a listening ear can make you feel ten times better about yourself! You are never alone and there are other people who have been through what you are going through. You deserve to talk about it and get support. You can also write in a journal, too. *Who are some trusted people you can talk to that can help you?*

3. Take Care of Yourself.

One thing that also really helped me was taking good care of myself. Instead of moping around the house,

I would get up and get ready for school, put on a cute outfit and do my hair. When you take care of yourself you feel better! Also, I would make a healthy breakfast because I've noticed that when I do, I have more energy and better concentration.

If you are going through a challenging time, this is the time to take even better care of yourself. You may not feel like it at the time, but it can help you feel much better later. *What are some ways you can take great care of yourself?*

4. Get Positive!

I'll admit, one of the things I didn't like doing at first, but which did help me a lot, was that I decided to look in the mirror and say positive things about my life and myself. I realized that even the littlest things can help make you feel better. Here are a few examples of things I would say:

"I love that I have pretty hair." "I love that I have great handwriting." "I am smart."

This is important because putting positive things in your mind can change how you feel. When I am talking negative to myself, I just want to lie around and do nothing. However, when I am positive, I get excited and I do great things like even writing this chapter in this book!

Right now, think about what are some things you are grateful for about yourself or your life? (It can be anything — something that brings a smile to your day, something you love, something about you that is unique, or someone who makes you happy!)

Life is not perfect. Sometimes life is hard and unfair. Everyone goes through tough times — EVERYONE. The good news is that you can make it through stronger and better than ever! How?

Remember: Times can be tough but *you are tougher!*

Stay active, talk to others about your feelings or situation, take care of yourself, and get positive! You'll see! You can tough it out and turn those tough times around!

Better Days Are Ahead!

By
Lexie Cunha

When I was younger, I felt like I could hold the world, but unfortunately that started to change as I got older.

Everyone goes through tough times at one point or another in life — everyone — including me.

For me, my tough times started in middle school. Many people saw me as the "weird girl." I was different. I was really small and wore glasses. I was really smart and passionate about things like Japanese animation and reading. I felt like I didn't "fit in." I guess I was easy for other people to pick on. It was never physical; it was the way they would look at me, avoid me, or the things they would say — but sometimes that can hurt more. It caused me to really question myself and who I was.

While bullying can be less of an issue as you get older, the impact on how you see yourself can continue to affect you long after you've left those middle school hallways. As you get bigger, sometimes the pressure can get bigger, too. There can be social pressure to look and act a certain way to fit in. There can be media pressure to measure up to an impossible beauty standard where you are supposed to have model-like appearances and very skimpy clothes. There can be peer pressure about choices like smoking, using alcohol or other drugs, and even pressure in relationships. If someone isn't careful, all of this pressure, on top of everything else going on, can add up to self-esteem issues and feelings that you are just not good enough, pretty enough, or smart enough.

That is exactly what happened to me. As I started high school, my mind was filled with all the ways that I didn't measure up. I felt that nothing could get better and that I wasn't what I thought I should be.

While I was often trying to smile on the outside, I was often crying on the inside as things kept getting worse and worse. I was keeping everything to myself.

On many days, I would retreat to my journal — my safe haven. It was a place where I didn't have to hide and act like everything was "okay." Acknowledging my feelings in my journal did help quite a bit. But with all the negative thoughts that continued to beat me up, just writing in my journal wasn't enough. I felt so alone.

Rather than continue to keep my struggles a secret, I made what I realize now was a crucial and powerful life-changing decision — the same decision that anyone struggling owes it to themselves to make. *I decided to talk with someone.*

I approached my good friend — someone I knew I could really trust. She is an amazing listener and is always helping her friends feel better. (She also has the best laugh that makes everyone around her laugh, too.) Even though I was scared, I let her know how down I was feeling — and I mean *really* down.

She looked at me with open understanding. She candidly told me that she had dealt with the same thing in her life, too. She went on to share some of her serious struggles and how she was able to make it through them, and how she now lives a better and stronger life because of what she went through!

She also said that even though tough times feel like they are going to last forever, tough times are temporary, and it is so important to keep pushing through because better and better days are ahead.

What?!?!? I was shocked. I couldn't believe that this beautiful and happy person in front of me would have ever struggled like me!

Hearing her story, something stirred inside. It was hope. It was a sense that I wasn't the only one. I wasn't alone.

Knowing that I wasn't alone made me feel so much better. She also told me that many people go though tough situations and feeling down at times. She talked about her own journey and how important it is to tell someone — a trusted parent, caring adult, or good friend. She said that anyone struggling deserves to get support through that situation — it is one of the biggest and most important steps up!

She also went on to say that she had decided to make the awesome choice to go to a counselor, who really helped her to deal with her situation and feel better. What an amazing way to stand up for yourself and your life!

As I emerged from months of fake happy faces that had hidden my silent struggles, my friend helped me to have the courage to talk to my mom and get some support. What I realized is that we don't have to deal with tough situations alone. Everyone deserves to have a success team — a team who is behind you every step of the way. Even if you feel alone, getting your own success team all starts with talking to someone you trust! Tell a counselor in your school, a trusted teacher, a caring family member, or a friend! Tell someone!

As I reflected on my friends, my mom, my counselor — this very diverse team of support — I realized I wasn't alone in the world anymore. I realized that even though things may feel like they are falling apart, things *will* be ok. Even though you feel really down, you *will* be able to get back up.

And I *did* start to get back up. Things *did* start to get better. Taking the steps to get back up after feeling so down wasn't easy, but let me tell you, *it is worth it!*

I decided that, just like anything, you have to practice and work for what you want. I decided to practice and work at *happiness!* In addition to getting support from my "success team," I decided to play a game — a game of positivity!

What do I mean? Well, before I made the life-changing choice to tell someone and put my struggles in the open, I used to retreat to my journal and only write down my negative thoughts. It helped, but the real turning point happened when I decided to use my journal to keep "score" on my positive and negative thoughts each day.

How did the positivity game work? At various times during the day — the morning, between classes, lunch, etc. — I would check in with myself and write down the meaningful thoughts that I had at that moment, both positive and negative.

At the end of the day, in order to keep score in my "positivity game," I'd highlight my thoughts in my journal with either a pink or yellow highlighter — pink for positive thoughts, yellow for negative thoughts.

The goal of the game was that I wanted to add more positives to my day, and if I got more positives than negatives, that meant I won the game that day! To do this, there needed to be more pink lines than yellow ones. Simple rules—but little did I know how they would change my mindset and my life!

At the end of the first day, I couldn't believe how much yellow highlighting there was. I was so surprised to see how much my negative thoughts were taking over my day. There weren't very many positives at all! No wonder I was feeling so down!

I said, "Enough is enough!" I knew if I wanted to get better at something, even positivity, I needed to practice. I made it a goal to add more positives every day. In order to do this, I started to practice positivity by consciously looking for the positives in different situations, even if at first they were frustrating. I started to look for the positives in other people, too.

The more I practiced looking for the positives, over time, the more my positive thoughts gradually started growing in number! My journal became more and more full of pink lines, and more importantly, I felt better and better.

The more positivity games that I won, the more I saw myself genuinely smile—and it wasn't just a smile from "winning" the game; it was because I felt good. Those thoughts that "nothing would ever change" actually started to change to "my life can get better and it *is* getting better."

As time went on, I looked at all those bright pink tally marks and the pink-line-filled pages in my journal and realized that I had to really search to find the yellow! It was a wonderful feeling!

In looking at my journal and my "positivity game," I realized that the game goes much further than that — life is actually a game, too. You just have to know how to play it. The game of life has twists and turns and ups and downs, but regardless of what space you are on, you can build up your positive points (your positive thoughts) and can trade them in in for amazing things: higher self-esteem, higher motivation, and the biggest thing is a good life overall. No matter how far behind you think you are, when you are able to look around and actually see the bright side, you can win on whatever space you are on!

With the support of my success team and my efforts to press forward to make it through, I'm amazed at how far I've come from those very down days. Looking at my journal now, years later, I don't even feel the need to highlight anymore. (My journals are filled with so much positivity that to highlight it all, I feel like I would be wasting my pink marker!)

I went from thinking, "I don't like myself; why should anyone else like me?" to, "I like myself; other people should, too, and if they don't, that's their problem."

While it took a lot of work and time, I can finally, truly say that I love me! I'm able to smile again, and if people ask me why I'm smiling, I don't always have an answer. I'm genuinely happy — I don't need a specific reason. Me, myself, and I are great. It's not about being arrogant — liking yourself means that you can be who you really are and be happy with that. It means that you can be alone in a room and still laugh. Happiness means you love you, and that is what really matters.

The great news is that if it's possible for me, it's possible for everyone — you, too! I realized that maybe one of the reasons I went through such a tough and difficult situation is so I can now help other people who are struggling, too.

Now please don't think that my life is suddenly perfect. Like everyone, my life still has its ups and downs, but I know now that's what keeps life interesting and helps you grow. I know that even though there can be clouds sometimes, if you keep going and you keep looking, you will get through them to see the sun.

Struggles happen to everyone — regardless of how perfect their life may look on the outside. The truth is, your life is never going to be 100 percent perfect — no one's is — but it is your choice to make it better. No one else can change it but you, and you don't have to do it alone. Everyone deserves support — including you!

If you ever feel really down or are struggling with a tough situation, make the decision right then to get up, talk to someone, and get support. Tell someone you trust. Talk to a trusted adult: a parent, a teacher, a mentor, a counselor, someone you look up to. Talk to your trusted friends, too. It starts with just telling one trusted person, and before you know it, you can have your own success team!

By talking to others, getting your feelings out, getting support and practicing positivity in your life, that frown — which you may feel is super glued onto your face forever — will start to peel off, a little at a time. And one day, you will look in the mirror and see a beautiful smile shining back — and it will be yours! That boulder that may feel like it is weighing you down will eventually feel like a pebble that you can pick off with a finger!

You will see! Your happiness will be so much more lasting!

Remember next time you are dealing with a struggle, even if it feels like things will never get better, remember that tough times are temporary — things <u>will</u> get better! With help, people do make it through to better times.

Ask for help. You can feel better. If you are struggling, you deserve support to get through this difficult time and to know that you are not alone. Take the first step now and talk to someone you trust.

Your future self and your brighter future will say "thank you!"

Better days are ahead!

Make Your Own Recipe for Friendship!

By

Isabella Eydelsteyn

My name is Isabella and I like to bake chocolate chip cookies with my mom.

One of the most important things about baking cookies is following a good recipe.

Good recipes make good friendships, too, but more about that later. Let's start with the cookies.

For our family recipe we include:

1 1/2 sticks of butter	2 1/4 cups of flour
1 large egg and 1 egg yolk	1 cup of packed brown sugar
2 teaspoons of vanilla extract	1/2 teaspoon of baking soda
1/2 cup of granulated sugar	1/2 teaspoon of salt

And, of course, 1 to 1 1/2 cups of semisweet chocolate chips

When we make the cookies, we preheat the oven to 325 degrees, melt the butter and let it cool slightly, and mix it with the vanilla and eggs using our electric mixer. We then sift in the dry ingredients while the mixer is turning and lastly we stir in the chocolate chips by hand.

I especially like to stir the dough. After we mix everything together, we take a large spoonful of dough and either push it directly onto the greased cookie sheet or, when we want all the cookies to look the same size, we roll the dough into balls about one and a half inches across and place them on the baking sheet. We like the cookies soft so we bake them in the oven for 13 to 17 minutes, and out come about two dozen gooey, warm, delicious cookies!

They taste really good! They are sweet, tasty and make me feel really happy.

Can you imagine what would happen if I used hot and spicy jalapeno sauce instead of vanilla? Can you imagine how the cookies would taste if I used dirt instead of flour? Yuck! With such a bad recipe, those cookies wouldn't be good at all.

Instead of making me feel happy, they would make me sick. And they might even bring tears to my eyes.

Why all this talk about a recipe for chocolate chip cookies?

I believe that just like it is important to follow a recipe for good cookies, it is important to follow a recipe for good friendships, too — whether you are in elementary school like me or actually at any age or stage of life.

I will share some examples of how good friendship recipes and bad ones have worked out for me.

The good news is that just like there is a recipe for an outstanding chocolate chip cookie, there is a recipe for a positive friendship.

Here is my personal friendship recipe:

2 large cups of trust

1 cup of love

100 drops of happy (good friendships are supposed to make you happy)

5 tablespoons of fun

1 1/4 cups of caring

1/2 cup of getting along

3 cups of defending your friend

1 pint of compliments

5 teaspoons of wisdom

7 cups of inclusion (making sure to include your friends in fun things that you are doing)

Then you mix all the ingredients together, give it a little time, and...you have a great friendship!

My best friend meets this recipe perfectly. She and I like to play all kinds of games together, we like to laugh, she makes me feel content, and I make her feel happy.

How do you know if you are using the right friendship recipe? Good friendships make you feel good about yourself and others and make you feel happy inside.

Good communication is another key to a close friendship. Even when my best friend and I argue, we can each talk about our points of view and we resolve our differences. I am always surprised how quickly my friend will forget about our disagreements — the next day we start fresh and have fun together. She is not stubborn; instead, she and I take turns being the one making the decisions about what we will play. I love that she appreciates my positive qualities and encourages me to be myself.

I care a lot for my friend and I look out for her. If someone is not being nice to her, I stick up for her and support her. My goal is to look out for her best interests and to make sure that she knows that I am there for her. This shows her that I love her and that she can trust me. I always feel better when I have time with my friend because we both have fun and feel close to each other.

Just as people can use a recipe for a good friendship — sadly, there are some who use a bad recipe for friendship. It's like adding dirt and jalapeno sauce to chocolate chip cookie dough. Yuck!

I recently experienced a classmate who was using a bad friendship recipe. In fact, I wouldn't even call it a friendship at all. She calls girls mean names and tries to make them feel bad about themselves.

Her recipe for friendship probably looks more like this:

5 cups of mean

1 gallon of bullying

1/4 cup of jealousy

2 cups of hurtful words

2 quarts of hate

When I was working with my group to complete a class project, my team thought I was helpful and doing a good job. I was the group leader and I believe that part of being a leader is to speak up in a positive way when it can help others. Most of my group was happy with my leadership; however, one girl in the group (the one whose recipe I mentioned) got jealous and said that I was doing a "bad, sassy job." She kept on calling me bossy, which hurt my feelings. Her comments brought tears to my eyes and made me feel like I didn't want to continue working on the group project. I felt hurt and sad but I was also worried that our group would not finish on time.

Then I realized, just as I wouldn't eat a cookie made of dirt, I didn't have to accept her comments made of jalapenos! I said to myself, "Don't focus on the bad. Focus on the good." I remembered all the positive things that my true friends say to me and how helpful they think I am. So I did not give up and I helped my group complete the project.

Why do some people call each other names? I think that sometimes they feel left out or jealous, or someone has said damaging things to them so they follow suit and say harmful things to other people.

In my opinion this is bullying. Don't listen to bullies. My mom told me that there is an old saying that goes, "Sticks and stones may break my bones, but names will never hurt me." But she and I both think that this old saying is not 100% true. Actually, name-calling really can hurt others, so it is important to surround yourself with people who are thoughtful, polite, and don't say hurtful things.

I prefer to spend my time with friends who have good friendship recipes! These friends encourage me when I'm feeling down and listen to my stories with interest. My true friends compliment me when something good happens to me and like the way that I lead.

I also know that in order to have close friends, I have to be a good friend, too. I follow my own recipe! I have a caring heart and want the best for people. I always try to be sensitive to how people are feeling, understand people's differences, and try to include everyone in a group.

In our gym class, another girl and I were always the last ones to be chosen for a team. I didn't want her or me to feel left out so I asked her to be my partner. That way we were both included and created our own team. It is important to think about other people and try to include them whenever possible.

What is your friendship recipe? Think about your friends. What kind of friendship recipes are they using? If one of your friends is saying that she doesn't want you to be part of her group or doesn't want you to play a game with her or seems jealous of you, watch out! That person may be a bully or someone who is not capable of being a good friend.

If you feel like you are being bullied, you can try to talk to the person who is making you feel bad and let her know how you feel. If the person cannot understand you or makes fun of you in front of others, then you will know that she is using a bad friendship recipe.

It may seem very hard, but it is important that you find other people who are able to be true friends. Sometimes it is difficult to reach out to new people or people you don't know very well. But if you are true to yourself and know that you deserve to be treated well, you will find new friends who follow good friendship recipes.

So what are some ways to reach out to others? You can ask someone to join in a game or activity you are doing, such as a book club. I share my books with my friends and let anyone, who wants to, look at them or read them. I also make friends when I take classes like gymnastics, dance, or swimming. Joining a soccer team each fall allows me to meet kids from many different schools.

Maybe you can join a new sport, try a new activity, or just say "Hi" to a new classmate. Look around! Great new friendships are everywhere!

Look for the good friendship qualities that are in your own recipe for friendships and cherish those friends. They will bring you joy and happiness and make your life sweet — even better than a chocolate chip cookie! ☺

Stand Up for Yourself!

— By —
Mirrah Jackson

My favorite color is rainbow with sparkles! Even though I'm little, I have big goals, big dreams, and a big personality! I also have big responsibilities, too, like helping at the fundraiser store at my mom's daycare called "Mirrah's Delites." I like fashion, swimming, baking and movies.

I like to be me — unique, smart and beautiful. It doesn't matter how old you are — you should like to be you, too!

Sometimes, me being me and you being you can be tough, though. It can be tough for so many reasons — because of a new situation, worries, fears or even sometimes, because of other people.

Before I started my new school, I was worried about making new friends. I wondered, "Would they like me? Would they think I was fun?"

I also worried, "Would they think I was funny like my other friends? (I like to laugh and make my friends laugh!) Would they think that I'm smart? Would they like that I have a caring heart and want to help others?" I really worried if I would fit in.

As I got ready to walk into my new school, I decided that instead of worrying about fitting in and what other people would think, I would just be me — smiles, smarts, laughter, and all! So even though I was really nervous, I tried not to show it. The class had twice as many students as my old school. There were so many new friends I could meet, so I was really nice and kind to everyone.

It worked, too! I met so many new classmates that day and they made me feel so welcomed! So many invited me to sit with them at lunch, it was even hard to choose where to go or who to play with at recess!

I made so many new friends — and as it turns out, they all liked me just as I was as my unique and beautiful me!

...Well, all except one!

She definitely was not happy about me being me, coming on her scene, getting attention and making new friends, who were her friends, too.

I thought she could be a friend too, but rather than being my friend, she became very jealous and mean and started to bully me. I didn't understand why she just didn't want to join in on the fun we would all have at recess or group time.

On the third day at my new school, I was sitting at my desk in homeroom playing and laughing with one of my new friends, while we were waiting for the teacher. The unhappy girl kept looking at me with a mad look on her face—I tried to ignore her, but it was hard.

In the middle of homeroom, she walked up to my desk and said, with a voice full of anger, "Mirrah, I'm going to hurt you!" and then later that afternoon, she actually hit me and called me mean names. I couldn't believe it! I sure wasn't used to someone being mean or not liking me.

Have you ever had something like that happen to you or someone you know?

I was so confused and felt really hurt. I couldn't believe that this happened! As I thought about what the bully did, I wondered why she would act like that. Why would she be mean to me for me just being me? Why would she be so hurtful when I was being so nice? Was it just because she was not happy about her friends now being my friends? This didn't make any sense!

The one thing I knew for sure is that physical violence or verbal abuse against me (or you!) is completely inexcusable and should never be tolerated or allowed, so I knew I needed to take the action right away—and not just any action, the right action!

I didn't hit her back. My mom told me to always tell the teacher first, and so I did. School was almost over for the day and the teacher told both of us to stay after class. She did not stay. When the teacher looked around for her, she had already left with the other students, so I just went outside to wait for my mom.

I was so hurt by the bully's words and actions; I couldn't wait to tell my mom what happened. When she saw me, she knew something was wrong. My face was red from being so mad and even my fist was balled up.

"What is wrong, Sweetie?" My mom asked with concern. I told her what the girl did to me.

After I told her what had happened, I was so glad that I did because she went right in and talked to the vice-principal about the situation. My mom helped me understand that anytime you are bullied or ever hurt by someone, you should never keep it to yourself and should always tell someone you trust right away. You deserve support and to be treated with respect! Everyone does!

I asked my mom, "Why would she do that? I thought she could be my friend." My mom explained that a bully, someone who makes you feel bad or someone who hurts you is not a friend. She said that, in my situation, the bully was probably jealous because her friends liked me; and that took some attention away from her. Rather than the bullying being about her not being happy with me, I learned that she was probably was bullying me because she was not happy with herself.

Unfortunately, even though the vice-principal talked to me and the bully, the bullying continued. The tough thing about bullying is that it hurts really badly, especially on the inside. She warned me to keep quiet and not tell anyone. I knew this was the opposite of what I should do. If someone is hurting you or being mean to you—ALWAYS TELL SOMEONE, ESPECIALLY AN ADULT YOU TRUST, RIGHT AWAY.

So, rather than keep quiet like she warned me, I decided that I would keep telling people—my teachers, my friends, and of course, my mom and dad.

As it turns out, the more my mom and I told people about what was happening, the more we learned that she was also bullying a lot of other students too—but I was the first one to really speak up and say something.

I'm so glad that I did, too! Because I decided to speak up and say something, I was able to stand up for myself and all the other kids who felt like they couldn't stand up for themselves.

My parents and I wouldn't stop until the bullying stopped! My mom showed me what it means to stand up for a cause! She met with the PE teacher, she met with the principal, she met again with the vice-principal, and even talked with the school board. When the bullying continued, my mom even had to threaten to get the police involved by pressing charges against the bully. That's when we learned that, at that time, our school did not even have any policies or rules against bullying.

Sometimes standing up for yourself and for what is right can be tough. While it's a pretty long story, things did eventually start to change and get better.

As a result of all the speaking up, the school put a "No Bullying Policy" in place.

The principal also put on our first school-wide anti-bullying rally to help everyone understand what bullying is and that bullying would not be tolerated.

Later, I even received an OK apology from the bully—but she eventually got suspended for all of the people that she was continuing to hurt. The bully learned that bullying comes with serious consequences.

I was still so understandably angry about the whole situation and couldn't figure out why it happened. My mother explained that sometimes hurting people hurt others. She said that the bully may have been going through something tough at home and suggested I try to have compassion for her.

After the bully was out for a few days, many of my classmates felt much safer and happier.

I am glad that I could make a difference in school...I can't believe that this all started from me standing up for myself, my right to feel safe and just be me.

I hope that my story helps and encourages you, too.

So what does this have to do with you? Just like I am me and you are you, we all deserve to be respected for who we are and treated with kindness. Anytime someone bullies you – verbally or physically, you should never keep it to yourself and always tell someone like a trusted adult and get help.

To make sure you are safe and free to be you, no matter how old you are or what situation you are in, here are some ideas to stand up for yourself and others, too!

Make a Commitment to Yourself:
No matter what type of situation you are in, make a commitment to yourself like, "I PROMISE to always report

any incidents or suspicions of bullying or abuse to my teacher, parent, mentor or trusted adult, when it is safe to do so."

Speak Up:

Speak up! If you are being bullied or have been hurt by someone, there is a chance that a lot of others are, too. Keep telling teachers, mentors, parents, or other trusted adults until someone listens! Don't be afraid to tell your mom or your dad or another trusted adult when you are hurting. You deserve to feel safe. (My mom is my hero for listening and teaching me how to take the correct action!!!)

If you are being hurt verbally or physically in your own home, school or other place, make sure to speak up and tell someone you trust right away.

Stand Up for Yourself:

Standing up for yourself means that rather than sink to the bully's level, you remember that bullies often try to make others feel bad because the bullies feel bad about themselves. If you were bullied, hurt or abused, standing up for yourself means remembering this is not your fault and that you did nothing wrong — it happened because there is something wrong with the bully.

There is never any excuse for someone bullying or hurting someone else, but sometimes bullies act out for reasons we can't see. Sometimes their bullying could be a cry for help or they are having trouble at home. People who feel truly good about themselves don't try to put down or hurt others.

Standing up for yourself also means remembering that regardless of what anyone else says or does, you are a good and valuable person, worthy of respect. It means taking the high road and continuing to treat others with respect too. It can also mean taking positive actions like talking to your principal about having a strong "No Bullying" policy to ensure you have a safe school environment or telling a school counselor about someone who hurt you.

It's good for me to be me and for you to be you! You deserve to be treated with respect and kindness!

By making a <u>commitment</u> to get help if you are being bullied, deciding to <u>speak up</u> and tell someone who can help, and remembering to continue to love and respect yourself and others, you will <u>stand up for yourself</u> and, in the process you will take a stand for others, too!

See the World with New Eyes!

By
Elizabeth Crow

Having been on a few different retreats before, I was expecting the usual. What I didn't realize was that this was no "normal" retreat...

This retreat was called a *poverty retreat* — an odd name, but anyone could guess we would learn about poverty. What I wasn't so keenly aware of was that I would be *living it*.

Before the retreat officially began, about 40 high school students, including me, were sitting with our friends at small round tables at the retreat center. The rumors were running around non-stop about what to expect about what was going to happen.

I overheard many conversations as we tried to scrape together what we knew and what we didn't:

"Well, they said we would be on a fast."

"I heard we were going to sleep outside."

"But the news said there was a storm coming! They can't make us sleep outside if there is lightning."

As I joined in, I found it fun to guess what we would be doing. We were joking about what would happen in the next two days and if we'd have to sleep under bridges.

We ate our dinner — plain rice and beans — and it was not that great. Some people found it gross, while others ate the whole meal knowing that it might be their last source of food for a couple days. When I had finished mine, I added my plate to an overflowing trashcan filled with half-eaten food.

We were called into the main room which was large and had a stage. The retreat leaders went over the rules and then, without explaining much, told us that we would be in teams that would have to compete. I thought that it was odd they would divide us into teams that, at the time, didn't seem to stand for much. Every team was given a third world country name and a stack of papers which each had a picture of a child, a name, and a story.

Again, with little explanation, we were told that these half sheets of paper were to be our new identities. We were told to hold on to the piece of paper all weekend because that would be important. Little did I know how important it would turn out to be...

At first, all of us were too focused on the competition to really think about the kid on our paper. A made up story of a little girl in a faraway location seemed so distant from my own life.

We continued with the activities. We had many experiences which resembled the plights of everyday people who are caught in poverty.

We did a "water walk" to simulate how those who live in poverty have to walk long distances to get water (which is not even clean the majority of the time). We also had to experience what it would be like to "escape our country" to simulate how some refugees must escape from their own homelands to avoid persecution. We even had to sleep outside in cardboard boxes to experience how many homeless people live every night. All the while we were not allowed to eat and constantly thought about food and how we were so hungry. It definitely started to have an impact on me.

All the while I had that little piece of paper tucked away in my pocket, barely giving it a thought—that is, until the last day of the retreat.

On this particular day, we were asked to take some time for personal reflection alone. This is an exercise where everyone goes by themselves to read and think about their experiences for about 30 minutes.

On this particular day, our directions were to take out the papers that were handed out at the very beginning of the retreat. All the students pulled out their long-forgotten papers, each with a different story, name, and face.

The retreat leader revealed, "You may think that is just a piece of paper, but the precious face of that child that you hold in your hand is real! Their identity is real. Their story is real."

I took a small gasp. I looked at the tragic story I had been carrying around with the picture of a smiling girl with sad eyes. I realized that this was not some made-up story to make me feel bad. I realized, at that moment, that she was someone real! The piece of paper was something I could empathize with. More importantly, she was *someone* I could empathize with. Her name was Millie.

As my stomach continued to rumble from fasting for about 30 hours, I decided that I had spent enough time thinking about my own hunger pains. I decided that it was time to think about hers— Millie's—and my own pains faded to the background.

As I sat against the cold stone wall, I read her story over and over again. It was so tragic, that at first I had difficulty even believing it was real. As I looked at the picture and her sad eyes, I began to see the truth of her situation and her story. I began to think about what it must be like to be her. She was only 11 and had seen more horrors and difficulties in her life than most do in a lifetime.

To me, she was no longer some piece of paper. She was not just some face. She was someone! She was precious, precious Millie.

By relating her story to myself and thinking and feeling what it would be like to be in her situation, I could feel my heart hurt for her and I was filled with compassion.

It was at that moment that I really learned what empathy is all about. More than just learning it – I also began to feel it. Rather than being focused on how hungry I was or the next activity, all I could think about was Millie and her suffering.

While I could not pretend to know the extent of her pain, I was moved by it. I realized that my hunger pains would be gone by tomorrow, but her pains might linger with her as a burden, for a very long time. I started to think about the fact that she was not the only one. Many girls may not have the same story but they are in the same situation. Because of where they were born and the circumstances they were born into, some girls in parts of the world may have very difficult times coming out of poverty and living anything close to the life I do today.

Far from being just a retreat — this was a transforming experience. Seeing the world through Millie's eyes gave me new eyes — eyes that let me yearn to see a person's story rather than just their condition.

It changed my perspective of people and the world. Before the retreat, coming from a wonderful home and great opportunities, I may have overlooked a homeless person on the street, or been a little scared, or may have judged that they are in that situation because of their own mistakes.

My eyes of empathy and compassion now help me see differently — maybe they were faced with a loss, tragedy, or some other situation that led them to those places. While it's not impossible, it can be difficult to escape poverty and I don't know their stories.

I realized that it doesn't stop there, either. I also started to use this mindset of empathy and compassion with anyone that I knew or met. I embraced the idea that it is not my job to judge someone because of their circumstances, but it is my job to help make their life better!

For example, at school, there was a girl who acted different than most people — some would say that she was socially awkward. Instead of doing homework during study hall, she would talk really loud and would sometimes talk about inappropriate things.

Before my retreat, I went with the crowd and would judge her as weird or rude. After the retreat, though, rather than judge her, I got to know her story and learned that she had autism, a condition that made it more difficult for her to communicate and connect in relationships. I now look at her with compassion and try to make her feel more included.

This mindset has made all the difference — it helped me become the more empathetic and compassionate person that I have always wanted to be!

Through empathy and compassion, you can appreciate how a simple dinner of rice and beans could be seen as a feast by people in other parts of the world. You can feel more grateful, be less self-focused, and less materialistic. It helps you become even more dedicated to being a leader and making a difference.

It doesn't just apply to homeless people, either, or those in poverty — it applies to everyone! You may not agree with someone's actions, choices, or situations, but don't judge the person. While every person is responsible for their own choices and actions, we all deserve to be seen as people rather than our circumstances.

It is also important that we see other people as people, rather than their places in life.

The same thing is true for you, too!

Take a moment to see the world with new eyes. Think about a person that you may judge. Think about what it must be like to be that person. What difficulties could they have faced that influenced where they are today? What are some of their worries? What may be some of their past hurts or regrets? If possible, how might you be able to help them or get them help in their situations?

See the world with new eyes — the eyes of someone else — and you go beyond the narrow line of sight involved in judgment and labels and gain something much more valuable! You gain a broader vision of yourself and others as sisters, brothers, and citizens of the world.

Rock It!

By
Jess Thor

"You are a rare and precious gift. You are the
only you there ever was or ever will be. You are
in this world to give your unique combination of
experiences and talents. No one else can ever
leave your fingerprints on this earth."

—Patti Thor (my mom)

I always questioned why I did not look exactly like the rest
of my family. They all seemed to have everything the same:
same hair, same eyes, same nose, same height. I was never
like that. There was one thing that was completely different
about me, and I could not change it.

119

"Why am I different?" I would ask my mother.

"Because you're special," she would answer, without having a clue that this bothered me.

This answer never made me feel good because it felt like "special" was a bad thing. No one else could see why this was a bad thing and that just made me feel like even more of an outsider.

People would always tell me that having this trait was a gift — something to be happy about. I could never see it. They would say that others would pay hundreds of dollars every year to look like me. I could never see why people would want this, much less pay money to have it. In my mind, what made me different made me feel like I didn't belong to my family. Why did I have to be "special"?

I just wanted to fit in with my family. While there were so many traits and characteristics that I shared with my three older siblings, I did not recognize them. I could only see the one thing that made me different, and I hated it — my blonde hair!

In our family photos full of brown hair, I would see my blonde hair stick out like a sore thumb. Again, I would think about how my blonde hair made me different — and that "different was bad."

I was born a true blonde. By the age of three, I had golden ringlets and was given the nickname Blondie. The sun would reflect off my hair during a bright day, and Mom would tell me that my hair was beautiful — a comment that bounced right off my blonde head and right onto the floor!

As my unhappy relationship with my blonde hair continued, any compliment about my blonde hair, in my mind, would secretly become a criticism that I would tell myself about how it was bad to be different.

As I continued growing up, I continued to glare at my blonde hair in the mirror — but all of this ended one fateful Halloween night.

I decided to dress up as the character of Dorothy from the movie *The Wizard of Oz*. This girl from Kansas, who was transported to a foreign land with her little dog, had what I always wanted — brown hair!

Because Dorothy had brown hair and I had blonde hair, I asked my mom for help to figure out how I could make it work.

"Why don't we use a temporary hair color to make your hair brown?" suggested Mom. "That way you won't have to find and wear a brown wig."

YES! I screamed silently as I nodded my head. My dream was coming true. I would have brown hair. I would finally look like I belong to my family — even if it was for just one night!

Mom put the brown coloring on my hair. The colorant had a strong smell. For most people it might be offensive, but for me it represented the joy of realizing a lifelong dream. I was finally going to fit in—I was going to be a brunette!

Radiating with happiness at my gorgeous brown locks, I bounded off to the living room, excited about my new look. As I plopped onto the couch to celebrate with my favorite TV show, the back of my head (now brunette) was toward the door.

The rest of our house was a flurry of activity as my siblings and some of their friends were getting ready for a big night of trick-or-treating.

"Nicole," I heard my sister's friend Megan calling for her. The call got louder and a little more frustrated in tone. Suddenly, Megan was right behind me, "Ni-coole!!"

I turned around to see what the commotion was about.

Megan looked me right in the eyes, a few inches from my face, surprised. "Woah! I thought you were Nicole. With your hair dyed, I thought you were your sister."

My mind shifted with a realization in that very important moment. "What? I'm *not* my *sister*. I'm Jess! I'm different! I'm *me!*" At that moment, I realized that while my blonde hair was different from the rest of my family's hair, it was also something that made me unique!

A realization settled into my heart for the first time. What makes me different is *good!* Rather than criticize my differences,

I should embrace them! Rather than ridicule something that makes me unique, I should "rock it!"

As I washed out the temporary brown color and the golden blonde began to shine back through, so did my appreciation of something that made me different. Whenever I was worried about something that made me stand out, my new motto became, "Rock it!"

After that Halloween night, when someone compliments me on my hair color, I smile and say thank you! I love my hair now! I rock it!

Maybe you don't have blonde hair, but you do have things about you that make you different. Whatever they are, remember this: Rather than ridicule your differences, rock it!

Maybe it's your height. Rock it! Maybe it's your smile. Rock it! Maybe it's your love of art or science. Rock it! Maybe it's your sense of style. Rock it!

Rather than criticize your differences, celebrate what makes you unique! This is what "rock it" is all about!

I've heard the phrase, "You were born an original; don't live like a copy!" This is so true! Over the years, I have learned that if you try to act or be just like someone else, people will not always notice you because they have seen it before.

If you rock all those unique qualities that make you, you — meaning you embrace them instead of criticize them — the happier you will be and the more confident you will be, too!

You are the only one in the world who is just like you!

What makes you different makes you unique, and what makes you unique is worth celebrating — Rock it!

Be a Woman of Influence!

———————— By ————————
Anni Keffer

"Are you a leader or a follower?"** This was one of my mom and dad's favorite questions to ask me whether I was eating dinner, doing homework, or getting ready to leave for school for the day.

I was around five when they first started asking this question, so even though I had no idea how to spell leadership or understand exactly what it was, I knew it must be important — and I would always respond, "I am a leader."

As I got older, I began to think about the significance of what was being asked and to grow in my understanding of what leadership is all about.

During my time in middle school and high school, I thought being a leader was mainly about taking an active role in leadership positions and being a leader in my youth group. It felt good that my peers saw me as a leader and as someone that they could look up to or go to for help. On one particular day in high school, my definition of leadership expanded dramatically!

On the personal side of my life, a situation came up and I asked my parents, "What should I do?"

"You always seem to be careful and really thoughtful about the decisions you make, Anni," my dad replied. "When you think about the impact that your choices will have on both yourself and others, you will know what to do."

He was right. I was careful about my decisions; however, I had never really considered the impact of my personal decisions on others before. "Why does it matter?" I asked him. "I mean, I'm living my own life. My personal decisions really only affect me, right?"

He said, "No, because people are watching you. The minute you decide to be a leader you become a person of influence. People watch every move you make. When you make a decision based on principle, whatever that principle is, no matter if it's good or if it's bad, people will often make those same decisions. And they'll also take it further and make other decisions based off of that same principle. What you do and the decisions you make influence so many other people beyond anything you could ever imagine."

My dad continued, "Being a leader is not about leading when you're asked or just when you know that others are watching. Being a leader is rarely about being up on a podium in front of a large crowd or having a leadership title. Real leadership is lived out in every choice of your life, even when there is no audience. Your choices as a leader ripple out to influence others in the world like waves, whether you can see it or not."

As I reflected on the wisdom my dad taught me, I remembered being a little kid and throwing rocks into a big pond to see how big of a splash I could get the rock to make. Do you remember doing this, too? I realized that each of my decisions were like a rock being thrown into the water of life, and the ripples after were like the people that are influenced by that one decision! Wow!

True leaders know that their choices—school, friends, work, personal or otherwise—impact others in big ways! Followers tend to let life happen to them or make choices without really thinking about the consequences or impacts.

You will never make a decision, whether good or bad, that won't influence at least one person. The bigger the decision, the more people you influence. The more you realize that leadership happens every day with *every choice* that you make, the more powerful you will become as a woman of influence!

I realized that, "*Are you a leader or a follower?*" is a question that I should be asking myself every single day of my life!

In order to help me continue my leadership journey as a woman of influence, I put together a leadership checklist that I can refer to when I'm in a situation where it would be easier to follow, but where I know that the right thing to do is lead. In those moments, I remind myself of this list because it represents the five key qualities that I believe make an influential leader.

Be a Woman of Influence Leadership Checklist:
1. You know what you believe.
2. You are willing to stand up for what you believe.
3. You don't change your core values to fit the situation you're in.
4. You are passionate.
5. You are willing to make a difference.

This list was especially useful when, on one particular day, I saw the media repeatedly glamorizing destructive celebrities and choices, and I was sick of it! I was tired of the messages that we as young people are fed on a daily basis.

There seemed to be no one standing up for us and letting us know that we could rise above the lies we were being told to believe.

I knew something had to be done, but I couldn't see what my role might look like...or if there was even anything I could do to influence the situation. I was just a small town girl, who was just 19 years old. Could I actually make a difference?

Thankfully I had my trusty "Woman of Influence Leadership Checklist!" So I thought through the situation with my list. Here is what I came up with:

1. **You know what you believe.**

   I knew what I believed. I reflected on the life-changing question that my parents started asking me so many years ago: "Am I a leader or a follower?" I knew the answer to this question, hands down.

   "I am a leader!" I said to myself and smiled.

   I believe that despite what the toxic media says with all their negative messages telling girls and women to set their bar low and dream small, girls deserve to know that it's awesome to be a leader and dream big. *Check!*

2. **You are willing to stand up for what you believe.**

   I realized that even though it can be difficult, I am the type of person who stands up for what I believe in, even if I feel like I have to stand alone.

Regardless of the people who doubted me, I knew I needed to stand up for my generation, and those to come – to let them know that it is beautiful to live your life with character and purpose and it's powerful to live with determination to change your world in whatever way fits your passion. *Check!*

3. **You don't change your core values to fit the situation you're in.**

   I've always tried to rise above negative peer pressure and to try to stay on the right path, and I knew that this was something I wanted to help other young women with, too. *Check!*

4. **You are passionate.**

   I've known my passion for a long time. My passion is sharing my message through speaking, teaching, and writing for my generation, especially women. This checklist item was a great opportunity to reflect on this passion, and it gave me such confidence in preparing for the last item on my checklist. *Check!*

5. **You are willing to make a difference.**

   One of my favorite quotes is from Gandhi who said, "Be the change you wish to see in the world." As I reflected on this idea, I thought, "I am willing to make a difference. It's one of the most amazing things you can do in life!"

The question for me was "How?"

Then, an idea hit me...

When I followed my "Women of Influence Leadership Checklist" — knowing what I believe, being willing to stand up for what I believe, not changing my core values regardless of the outside world, reflecting on what I am passionate about and following that up with making the choice to make a difference — something amazing happened!

I decided to create my own event for girls called the "Young Women of Influence" event!

Even though I was only 19 — and many people thought someone like me couldn't put on my own event — in six months, I created an event from start to finish that brought young ladies together to learn about leadership, self-image, and goal setting. The road was not an easy one and it was filled with plenty of ups and downs and moments when I wanted to quit.

Thankfully, my focus on the five key qualities of leadership from my checklist kept me going — especially the last one! I knew that if I could change just one person's life with the messages presented at the event — just one — then everything it took to get there would be worth it.

The girls at the event spent the day hearing positive, uplifting messages about leadership and what it means to be a woman of character. It was one of the most rewarding things I've ever done, and it had a huge impact! Many of the girls who had arrived earlier in the day, with frowns and shoulders slumped under the weight of self-doubt, left with their heads held high and their hearts full of encouragement for the future.

It was so successful that I am now preparing for my next event and even launched a speaking career where I speak at schools, conferences, and other events on leadership and identity!

All of this started with one simple question I first heard so many years ago, "Are you a *leader* or a *follower?*"

My question for you is how would you answer that same question?

In the end, leadership is a *daily* choice. Anyone can choose every day to stand up and be a leader – including you – and maybe you already do!

It's about getting up each morning and saying, "Today, I'm going to be a leader. I'm going to make the right decisions. I'm going to keep sticking with the principles I believe in. I am going to make a difference."

What type of impact do you want to have? How can you put the five principles to work in your life as a leader and woman of influence?

Right now, think about a particular situation where you think you can make a positive change. It can be about something in your life, your school or community. Now, take a moment to go through your own "Be a Woman of Influence Leadership Checklist."

Your Own "Be a Woman of Influence Leadership Checklist:"

1. **You know what you believe.**

   What do you believe? In this situation where you can make a positive change, what do you believe is right? What are you going to choose: leading or following?

2. **You are willing to stand up for what you believe.**

   Are you willing to stand up for what you believe? Remember the earlier idea of throwing rocks into a pond. In this situation are you willing to stand up and make a positive influence—a splash—in the lives of others?

3. **You don't change your core values to fit the situation you're in.**

   Being a woman of influence and standing up for what you believe can be hard. As you try to make positive change, how will you react to others who may try to influence you in a negative way? Will you bend to the pressure and change your core values or will you stay strong?

   Dr. Martin Luther King, Jr. said, "The ultimate measure of a man is not where he stands in moments of comfort and convenience, but where he stands at times of challenge and controversy." What will you do to stay strong when there are obstacles or if people criticize you for doing the right thing?

4. **You are passionate.**

What are you passionate about changing for the better? This is so important! Pursue your passion...and let others be positively impacted through it. Pursuing your passion is a journey that will not only change your life, but also the lives of others. A lot of times we're afraid that if we're too passionate about something, people are going to criticize us. Actually, your passion can often draw people towards you in a positive way. When you know what you believe, you have integrity in each area of your life. When you're passionate, you're going to bring a lot of people with you. That's influence. That's leadership.

5. **You are willing to make a difference.**

Are you willing to make a difference? What are some positive ways you can do this?

As you answer this last question remember — everyone's path in changing the world is going to look different. Your journey to creating a positive impact on our world will be special and different compared to your friends, your parents, your siblings and even mine. That is the most wonderful part! We can each put our own unique stamp on the world.

You can choose to be a woman of influence by leading every day of your life. Being a leader doesn't mean you always have to be in the front or in the spotlight either—it means you stand on your principles and do what is right—regardless of who is watching. It can even start with small things you do every day! When you live as a leader, it will have a big effect on your own life and it will have a ripple effect far beyond what you can ever imagine!

Think about this question one more time: Are you a leader or a follower?

A leader of course!

Be a woman of influence!

Be Amazzzzzing At Any Age

——————— *By* ———————

Maya Baltinester

Amazzzzzing is one of my favorite words. It means to be not just amazing, but *extra* amazing!

I like to think that I am an amazzzzzing person. So are you, too! We actually all are amazzzzzing in our own way.

One thing that makes me amazzzzzing is that even though I am in middle school, I am the successful CEO of my own company.

My company is called Maya's Golden Artwork. I create and sell unique and special art, including drawings, paintings and even sculptures I make out of crayons. I even got a request for a commissioned piece of artwork from a celebrity! How awesome, right?

Some people might think that being in middle school you are too young to have a company. I believe that if you want to have a company or set another big goal and someone says you are too young, tell them:

"Who you are is not how old you are, you can be amazzzzing at any age!"

When you embrace this, amazzzzing things can begin to happen!

How do I know?

Well, recently I went to a special conference for business owners to learn how to bring my website to the next level. I attended this conference with my mom, dad, brothers and sister.

There were over five hundred people in the hotel ballroom at this conference! In the beginning I felt really weird and a little scared because everyone was a grown up. I was the youngest of all the participants.

At first, I was really quiet at the conference. I didn't speak up much because I was the youngest and felt shy. I didn't talk to many people either. After the first three days of the conference passed by, though, I couldn't keep the amazzzzing part of me inside quiet any longer.

On the 4th day of the conference when they played music after lunch to get the crowd energized, like they did every day, rather than be shy and just watch the adults dance on stage—I remembered that anyone can be amazzzzing at any age—including me!

I decided to join them and jumped up on stage! I let the best of me out to dance and my outgoing personality took over! I had so much fun dancing and laughing! I felt amazzzzing!

It didn't stop there! I became much more outgoing in the rest of the conference too! I had so much more fun at the conference and learned a lot. I enjoyed talking to so many people. Even though they were older, there were a lot of people I felt like I could connect with. I even handed out my business cards, designed my own website featuring an oil pastel picture of a jar with branches and leaves, and had people sign up for my web marketing campaign. Pretty amazzzzing, huh?

On the last day of the conference, I didn't even want to leave! That day was really special because they gave out awards— including "The Most Energetic Player Award." This award was given to the person at the conference who had the most energy.

As the speaker announced the top five qualifiers for this special award—I couldn't believe that one of the names was me!!!

I made the decision that if I won, I would do something amazzzzing — a cartwheel down the isle as I ran up to accept my award! I was no longer shy as I let me be myself!

When they announced the winner, they said, "Congratulations to Maya!"

I was so excited, that I did a cartwheel and went up on stage! My friends and family were standing and cheering! They were so happy!

I couldn't believe how I went from being one of the most shy people at the conference to being one of the most outgoing people at the conference all by deciding to let the amazzzzing part of me shine!

It was really fun to be on stage receiving the applause, but what I loved most was what I was able to give! As I stood in front of five hundred cheering people, I spread my arms out wide because it was a way to give love and I gave a big hug to the audience. It is an amazzzing moment that I will always remember!

You can have some amazzzzzing moments in life too — when you learn how to be you and let who you really are shine through. Regardless of how old you are, where you come from or what you've been through in life, you can be successful if you remember to be who you really are — someone pretty *AMAZZZZING!*

Get Booked for Success!

By
Demiya Miller

"Me, an author? I'm only 11! I've never even met an 11-year-old author!" I thought. "Is that even possible?"

I soon learned the answer to that question!

My mom, Andrea Adams-Miller, is a speaker and she gets to go to a lot of seminars and conferences. I always wondered what they were like and what they did there—also, I admit, I missed her when she left.

So when I learned about an upcoming trip to an event in Los Angeles, I begged my mom to go. I also wanted to go to spend time with my mom and because, well, Los Angeles equals celebrities! I thought it would be fun to meet some famous people, too.

She smiled and said, "Demiya, this is a business seminar and the only way I can justify taking you out of school to have this educational experience is if you decide to start your own business or write a book."

When she gave me the choices to start a business or write a book, I didn't know what to do. I had no clue how to start a business, but I had read books before, so I asked myself, "How hard could it be? I'm going to do this and whatever my message, I want to have a positive impact too!"

And with that, I completed the first step to reaching my goal of becoming an author and sharing my message! Whatever your goal is—whether it is to be an author or something else—I believe that anytime you set goals and try to be your best—you can positively impact the world through your words, actions and example.

Here's how!

Step 1: Decide!

Writing a book, sharing your message or setting any goal, starts with one simple but important choice—make a decision! I decided to become an author, even though, at first, I didn't know how it would turn out. With this first step and my mom's help, I sat down to begin the next steps of the book writing process.

Step 2: Choose!

Once I decided on my goal to become an author, I had to choose what specifically to do next to make my goal a reality! I tried to be realistic with my focus and do something that wouldn't be too big of a project to finish. I sat down with my mom to choose my topic and brainstorm what I could possibly write about that would be interesting. I wanted to write a non-fiction book that would help people. I realized that when you are an author it's important to write about something that you are good at or care about. I knew I was smart and had good friends and a great relationship with my parents, so I started there. Also, because I only had a month to write the book before the seminar, I decided to write a short "tip book" for pre-teens on how to succeed in school and in life. The tips would make it easy for my readers to follow the helpful advice—and easier for me to write it too!

Step 3: Create!

After I made a choice on what to do, it was time to create! The creation process is all about taking action! I started with coming up with the tips for the book. I knew I couldn't think of more than forty and I knew from overhearing my mom's business audio recordings that the number should end in 7, (because 7 sells better than any other number when it comes to business). I thought 37 tips seemed way too much and 17 weren't enough. That left me with the number 27; it was just the right amount! After I decided on the number 27 and came up with my book title, I began writing the tips. I just thought of what I did for school, what I did for home and what I did for friendships and other areas of my life.

Step 4: Connect!

As you are working towards any goal, it's important to connect! After a lot of connecting with friends and family, idea sharing and asking for help, I confirmed my book's title, *The 27 Preteen Tips to Get Good Grades, Get Good Friends, and Get Your Parents to Say 'YES' to Almost Everything.* Kids loved the title! As I worked on the book, I knew just like the title, the cover had to connect too because people often do judge a book by its cover. I tried to think of my audience—the kids who would be reading the book. I chose a notebook for the cover since the book had to do with school and I asked the graphic designer for help to add details to make it colorful and noticeable. I also realized that it was OK to get help too. Because typing is not one of my strengths, my mom helped me type them out as I put my list together.

Step 5: Promote!

As with any goal that involves having an impact, it's important to get the word out to others you may be able to help!

Now that my book was done, it was time to get it in print! My mom was able to help me get my book published. When

I saw the first copy of my book, it felt so amazing seeing it in print! I couldn't believe that I was a published author at 11 years old! I felt so proud that I would be taking the books with me when I traveled with my mom to the event in L.A.! I was excited to go.

The airplane ride there was very long, but they had a TV on the plane and some free snacks. As someone who often felt shy, I admit I was nervous on the plane as I thought about the event in L.A. I knew that I would be going to the seminar with my mom who knows everybody, and I would meet many new people.

At the seminar, my mom and I made a lot of friends who complimented me on my book. They were amazed I had written a book at such a young age. At the seminar, my mom introduced me to the person leading the seminar, James Malinchak. He is a leading authority on helping speakers and businesses to become successful. He is also famous and has been on TV and authored many of his own books. When he saw my book, he gave me a high-five!

Later during the event, when he was on the stage talking in front of over 600 business owners, I was so surprised! He started to talk about me and how I took the initiative to write my own book and become an author!

He then invited me to join him up on the stage. I was afraid I would hyperventilate because I have stage fright and there were hundreds of people staring at me! I was so nervous! As I stood next to him, he told the story of how I wrote a book to earn the privilege to come to his event. Then he told people in the audience that they could write a book to help people, too, since I had already written a book when I was just 11. Everyone laughed, but you could see in some of their faces that they wished that they would have had their own book done. Later, many said I inspired them to finally write their own books to help people, too. This made me feel really happy!

I also decided to use what I learned in the seminar after I got back home. From what I learned at the seminar, I was not yet done with my book writing experience. I realized that I could help more kids by writing an entire system to go with my tip book including an action guide, a journal, and a calendar, too!

When James heard about how I implemented his strategies, he was so impressed and surprised me by inviting me to come to his next event, to speak to his audience, and promote my book program at his event, too!

So the next time I flew out to L.A., it was as an author AND a speaker for the business conference! I'd come a long way from when I first started! As a speaker for his event, when I went up on stage, I was still extremely nervous. I was in front of 750 people or more and I was the youngest speaker, by far. I took a deep breath and focused on helping the audience understand my story and the process I used to write my book and student success system. After my talk, I got a standing ovation! Many people rushed to my book signing table to buy my book and program.

It was an awesome feeling that people actually wanted to buy my book resources. After many compliments and autographing so many books, I learned that I had sold out of all my books. I was so happy and felt so accomplished because a normal person like me could do something that stood out and was going to help the world.

With all the money I had earned, I felt like I could buy a brand new car or something! Actually, I had never had that much money before. For a while, I had been saving up for a new computer and realized that with the money from my book sales, I had just enough to get it!

Step 6: Give Back!

I was so happy for reaching my goal and completing my book. The next day of the conference, I was still glowing with how well things went the day before. James then talked about a special organization that helps kids become leaders and how they were raising money to give scholarships to disadvantaged kids who would never otherwise get to have that opportunity. He then had one of the program participants, I'll call him Jesse, talk about how he had been very mistreated as a kid and how the leadership program changed his whole life. As I listened to Jesse share his story, I was so moved by what he said and realized that I wanted to be able to impact someone's life, (someone just like Jesse) more than I wanted a new computer.

So even though it was a challenging decision, I knew it was the best one I could ever make for myself—I made the choice to donate all the money from my book sales at the event to help give scholarships to kids like Jesse.

Even though I was disappointed to know that it might take me a whole year to earn the money for the computer again, my heart was so happy that I was able to help hurting kids and youth get a better life.

Besides, good things happen to those who wait, right?

How true that is!

While I didn't expect it, a few weeks later, right before Christmas, I got a box in the mail from James. At first I was confused. I thought it might be some materials from the conference. But then I realized the box was the same shape and size as the new computer I had always wanted! I started freaking out in my head, but I wouldn't show my excitement on the outside just in case I was mistaken.

I wasn't! James sent me a nice note telling me he was so proud of me for donating to the student leadership organization that he wanted to reward me for my actions of helping others by sending me the brand new computer! I was speechless and very grateful. Good things do come to people who wait (and give back to others!)

Things got even better! Later, my mom suggested my sister and I apply to go to the student leadership event sponsored by the organization I donated to. Both my sister and I were accepted and invited to go for free! I was even asked to be interviewed for a magazine, and was interviewed on a TV show called "People Making a Difference!" The show is seen by over 4 million viewers! The list of amazing opportunities goes on and on—and continues! As you decide and achieve your own goals, think about how you can give back and help others too.

I know that without that very first decision to write my book, my life would be very different.

I realized through this journey that it's the small choices you make every day that add up to a big difference in the future! I had no idea that so much would come from the simple decision to be an author.

The same is true for you and your goals! Think about your life right now and one of your own goals.

Maybe you have a goal to write a book, start a club, run for a leadership position or you have a message that you can share to help encourage and inspire others in some way!

What are you waiting for? Remember to...

Decide!
Think about your life right now. What is an important goal you have? Make a decision on what you want your next goal to be and decide to go after it! Better yet, write it down right now!

Choose!
Regarding your own goal, choose what are the main steps you get to do next to make your goal a reality. To get you started, right now write down even just the smallest step you can take toward reaching your goal.

Create!
Take action! Jump feet first into the process of creating and making your goal a reality!

Connect!
You never have to work on your goal alone! Who can you connect with to support you with achieving your goal?

Promote!
Regarding your goal, think about who can be helped by learning about your goal, project or achievement — even if it is for them to be inspired by your story! It's OK to let others know that you did something awesome — as long as it is done from a place of caring and sharing.

Give Back!
After you've achieved your goal — or while you are working on it — think about some ways to "pay it forward" and give back

to others. Maybe it's mentoring someone else to help them reach their own goal, donating a portion of the proceeds you receive to an important cause or speaking to others about your story to inspire them to go for their own dream!

Get started and get booked for success!

Know the Truth About True Friends

——— By ———
Sarah Poche'

I could tell many stories about the summer that I was rushed to the hospital where, weeks later, I was diagnosed with a rare auto-immune disease. I was prescribed many medications including a very high dose of steroids that made me feel angry, confused and, if that wasn't enough, I gained a lot of weight. That is a lot for an 11-year-old to deal with. So much for my summer vacation!

I can't even remember most of my hospital stay, but I definitely remember what happened *after*.

Getting out of the hospital felt like a whole new world. I was totally FREAKED OUT! While I spent my summer in the hospital, all of my friends spent theirs doing normal summer activities. Even though my life was turned upside down, all my friends were living normal lives with no abnormal weight gain, no emotional outbursts, and no crazy nightmares.

I felt very isolated and alone. So many questions were going through my mind: What will they think of me when they see me again? Will they still want to be my friend? Will they accept me just as they did last year?

I kept worrying about what my friends would think of me. Finally, I realized that worry wasn't going to change anything. Instead of sitting around worrying, I decided to ask my mom for help in making plans with one of my best friends, Abby. Even though I have known Abby since I was four, I was a little nervous that she might react differently to me than she did before.

My mom set up a get together with Abby — my first time seeing any friend since I left the hospital. I looked forward to seeing Abby but I still worried, "What will she think about how I've changed?"

Days flew by and I continued to get better and stronger. The big day to see Abby finally arrived and I woke up thinking, "I can't wait to see her!" But as the day went on

I felt gradually more nervous. I started worrying, "What if she doesn't want to see me?"

By the time we arrived at her house I was even more nervous. "Would she still want to be my friend? Will she still treat me the way she did before? Will we still have fun together?"

My mom and I walked up to the front door of Abby's house and rang the doorbell. My heart was tense with both excitement and worry! Thankfully, all of my worry started to melt when Abby and I saw one another. Our eyes met and we both smiled.

Because so much time had passed and all the changes I had been through, we were both a little shy at first. I'm sure she had a lot of questions.

As we talked, it began to feel like no time had passed at all. She was Abby, my best friend — the same best friend before I had my hospital ordeal and the same one after!

By the time Abby and I had to leave, we were begging our parents, "Please, don't separate us!" (With us two girls running around laughing, giggling, and making a bunch of noise — her little brother was probably eager for me to go home, though!)

As the day ended and I was riding in the car on the way home, I realized something very special about true friendship: If people are your real friends they will love you no matter what. They will love you no matter what you've been through.

They will love you regardless of your shape or size. They will love you for you.

As I thought about seeing my other friends and going back to school for the first time since my health scare, my worried frown was replaced by a warm smile. I knew that if they were my real friends, they would love me with the same warmth and love that Abby did!

And they did! It was surprisingly easy when I saw them for the first time after that summer. It was like no time had passed between us. They were the same friends I had always had—the same personalities, humor, and everything. I realized how grateful I was to have true, genuine friends! Their support and acceptance made me feel so happy. All those worries I had before faded away!

It's not only about my friends and me—take a moment to think about your friends and you right now.

Do your friends love you just the way you are, or do they want you to change? Do your friends value your uniqueness, or try to bully you because of how you may be different? Do your friends try to boss you around, or do they care about your ideas?

If they don't accept you for you, they are NOT real friends! Distance yourself from them, and get closer to some real friends.

You deserve true friends! Why? Because true friends are one of the greatest things a happy life is made of!

Even though you may go through tough times or changes, one thing always remains the same: Your true friends are the ones that love you for you and accept you exactly as you are – and that's the truth!

Be a Class A.C.T.

By
Brittney Krempl

"Be a class act!" This is something I've always worked to be — someone who is admired, inspires others and stands out as their absolute best.

However, as the youngest child in my family, sometimes I felt it was hard to stand out because I have two other sisters who are quite a bit older than me and are very accomplished.

In fact, sometimes as the youngest, I used to feel frustrated — like I was living in the shadows of my sisters. I would feel like I didn't measure up or would fall behind as I constantly tried to be as good as they were.

More often now, though, I feel empowered and even happy about my place in the family. I feel like a leader. I feel like a *class act!*

How did this happen? I realized that whether I felt like a leader or a loser depended on if I decided to step up and be a "Class <u>A.C.T.</u>" in the situation!

What do I mean? Anytime you feel "less than" and like you don't measure up, you can choose to be a "class A.C.T." too!

A: Appreciate the Situation. I know this can be hard to do, but it is a powerful first step. Rather than thinking about all the negatives of being the youngest, I thought about what I can appreciate about having older siblings. For example, I focused on how my sisters gave me helpful advice about overcoming my fears about starting high school. I thought about how I was able to talk to my sisters about classes, teachers, and extracurricular activities. I also appreciated the fact that it was so helpful to have a sister to talk to whenever I felt stressed. Now, both of my sisters seem more like friends than sisters. I love being able to trust them and ask anything that is on my mind. Their advice is good and is exactly what I need to hear!

C: Consider Your Own Uniqueness. I also decided to consider how I was unique and different from my sisters and how that was a *good thing*. Rather than try to be exactly like them and live in my sisters' shadows, I decided to go on my own path to pursue achievements and goals that I find interesting. I thought about how, even though we are sisters, we are all unique individuals, too and I should never try to be someone else because I am best at being me!

T: Think and Know That You Are Just as Valuable! Instead of being frustrated when my parents talked about my sisters and their successes, I realized that my parents brought up my sisters' achievements as a way to help me be successful, too! I remembered that my parents do these things out of their love and care for me and that they love me and my sisters just the same. We don't have to compete—each of us has our own unique set of talents and gifts and our own place in life that supports one another and our family. While I am different from my sisters, we are all equal. Each of us can be a leader in our own way. Even though one of us may be better at something than the other, each of us is incredibly valuable just as we are!

The same is true for you.

Even if you are not the youngest in your family or you don't have brothers and sisters—you may be in a situation where you feel like the "most junior" or "least valuable" member of a team, a group or a club. Anytime you feel you are in a situation where you don't measure up, you can still decide to be a "class A.C.T.!"

Appreciate the situation, **C**onsider your own uniqueness and **T**hink and know you are just as valuable as everyone else.

Trying to be a "class A.C.T." each day can help you deal with unwanted comparisons in all areas of your life. Make sure to stay positive and to react to things in a thoughtful manner — this may help you, your outlook, and your relationships more than you think. (Talking things over with other people you care about and trust can be helpful as well.)

Keeping things in a positive perspective, recognizing how special you are and embracing your inherent value just as you are, right now, will help you lead your best life!

Be a class A.C.T!

See the Upside of the Situation

— By —
Sophia Waldenberg

The thought amazed me. I was astounded that one day I could be in the comforts of Washington State and the next in the tropics of Costa Rica. I stood at the exit of the airport in San Jose, Costa Rica, while the humid air caused my shirt and jeans to stick to my skin. I definitely had butterflies in my stomach. The idea of moving to another country for a year for a cultural educational experience—without knowing the language—had me excited, but nervous. Questions raced through my mind, *What will my new school be like? Will it be hard to make new friends? How will they understand me? How will I fit in?*

Two days later, I found out!

I began my 9th grade year as a freshman at The European School. Now, the first day of school — especially high school — for any girl, anywhere, can be completely nerve racking. Because I didn't know how to speak Spanish, I felt as though I was really in over my head! As I walked into the school, I remember seeing a lot of unfamiliar faces looking at me.

A new student came up, smiled, and then kissed me on the cheek! I was so shocked — the whole situation felt so weird! I didn't know what to do! Seeing my surprise, another student said that it is a custom to greet people by kissing them on the cheek, instead of shaking their hands. Wow. I didn't expect that.

Although everyone in my class seemed nice, at first it was very hard to make new friends because most of the kids had grown up together. I'm the kind of girl that is used to having a lot of friends and a big friend circle and lots of people to talk to when I feel stressed or uncomfortable. Their strong bonds made it difficult for me to get close to them. Combine this with the language barrier, and it made it more than challenging. I found that, while normally talkative, I didn't talk as much because I was worried about saying something wrong and them not understanding me.

On top of that, my little sister's transition seemed so easy! Even though I knew that the younger you are, often the more accepting kids are of you, it still bugged me that I was trying just as hard to fit in and wasn't making a lot of friends. It was awkward for me to feel like an outsider.

And it didn't stop there! The schooling system was also a whole new world. I was very used to my American public school back home—wearing my own clothes, medium to large class sizes, acing my homework and tests, and feeling like I fit in. The European School was like another planet—one with uniforms, small class sizes, super-high expectations, hard tests, and tons of homework. I was used to doing well in school without even trying, so the sudden change of events didn't sit so well with me, either.

I couldn't help but let my thoughts drift to all my friends that I had left in Washington and how they were enjoying their freshman year.

I wondered, *Did I make the wrong choice by agreeing to come here?* The more I entertained thoughts like this and the more I focused on the things I missed by being in Costa Rica, the more upset and frustrated it made me. I realized very quickly that focusing on those things was getting me nowhere!

So I decided to try to change. Instead of focusing on the things I missed or that made me feel down, I decided that I would try to see the upside of the situation.

It wasn't easy at first, but I kept trying—and trying—and trying!

165

As the days turned into weeks, at first, not much seemed to change. But gradually, ever so gradually, things started to change in a bigger way than I could have ever expected!

By trying to see the upside of things each day, over time I was actually growing to embrace the changes in my life!

By focusing on the upside of learning how to speak a new language, I thought how awesome it would be to know how to speak Spanish. Even though I felt so awkward at first, I devoted myself even more to my SSL class (Spanish as a second language) in school. I began to accept that while speaking Spanish was hard, especially in public, that the only way to get better and become fluent is to get over what people think and just practice out loud. I started to learn more and more quickly and spoke Spanish better and better!

By focusing on the upside of my new school, I thought about what a privilege it was to go to a school that had such a great focus on college preparation and I threw myself into my studies. Eventually it payed off in my grades! With the classes that were hard at first, I made the choice to see them as a challenge, learning to rise to the occasion and studying harder, and I started to ace my classes.

By focusing on the upside of not knowing many people, I thought about how awesome it was to be able to make new friends in a new country and I decided to join after school clubs and sports teams to meet new people. I joined the soccer team because I had played soccer for a while in Washington and decided to try it out again for fun.

I even decided to try new things that I would have normally never tried before! My friend Sarah and I joined the fencing club. Fencing was such a fun thing, and I'm glad I got involved in it. I grew to really like it because it was so different from other sports I'd done in the past. We also joined a dance team at a dance studio, so I met other girls from other schools.

The more I focused on the upside of making new friends, the more confident I was and the more I could reach out to others without feeling awkward and make friends no matter what the situation! I even adopted the fun custom of greeting people with a kiss on the cheek!

I realized that once you take time to focus on the upside of a situation, life can open up to you, and experiences you didn't think could happen, will.

By the end of quarter break as my family returned to Costa Rica from our two-week traveling adventures exploring Nicaragua, I realized that I was looking forward to seeing my friends and was amazed at how far I'd come by focusing on the upside of things.

School, speaking Spanish, and making friends all continued to get easier. Between sports, school, and going to the beach on the weekends with my new friends I finally felt comfortable living in this new country. I finally felt like I truly belonged!

I was also able to appreciate more and more about different languages, my passion for traveling, and understanding people of other cultures.

As my time abroad drew to a close, I realized that this experience taught me more in one year than in all my years of school put together.

Living in Costa Rica and learning how to focus on the upside of my experiences taught me so much — it helped me grow, shaped me into a better person, and taught me amazing things that I can use the rest of my life!

The good news is that you don't need to wait until you live in another country for a year to benefit from living life by looking at the upside of things.

You can try to look at the upside of a situation wherever you are right now, and it can help you learn from it, get through it, and grow in the process — whether it's moving to a new school, going through a tough time, auditioning for a play, joining a new club or team, or getting a new job.

It doesn't matter how perfect someone's life may seem, everyone goes through down times or may feel awkward as they are faced with a new situation.

Remember to keep moving forward, stay focused on what you want, and rather than let a situation start to drag you down, take a moment and see the upside!

Overcome
A Mountain
of Self-Doubt

— *By* —
Emmeline Whitcomb

The biggest mountain I've had to conquer in my life was a mountain of "self-doubt."

What started off as more of a hill started to really grow during elementary school when I had a teacher who, unknowingly, whittled away almost every ounce of my confidence. The simple joy I had as a child was buried under piles and piles of worry, fear and self-doubt.

I feel so grateful that up to that point in my life, I had amazing teachers—they had reputations for being "warm and fuzzy," kind, and encouraging but unfortunately the teacher in question, who I'll refer to as "Ms. Klotz," clearly was not.

I was a good student—I followed the rules and always turned in my homework—so getting yelled at and being picked on was not one of the things I experienced much. But I had my share of it that year.

I remember feeling ridiculed when she publicly labeled me as a "worry wart" in front of the whole class and yelled at me for even the smallest of mistakes. At one point, after talking with her privately about my concerns for a student who was doing things that were dangerous, she betrayed my confidence and disclosed our conversation to my classmate, adding "tattle tail" to my list of labels. I was devastated and afraid the student, who wasn't known for being nice, would bully me. After that incident, I never shared secrets with people other than my close family. The combination of these events and others often caused me to cry late into the night until my head pounded for fear of what the next day might bring.

There was a particularly traumatic day I will always remember. We always had short daily assignments. If we didn't finish, we could complete them at lunch and leave the work in a blue bucket outside the classroom...so long as we remembered to pick up the work before class started again. One day, I wasn't able to finish my daily assignment, so I held on to it, finished it at lunch, left it in the blue bucket, and went on my merry way to play for the rest of my free time. But when it was time to go back to class, I forgot to pick up my assignment.

It was the first time I had ever made this mistake. Many other students had forgotten to pick up their papers in the previous weeks as well, and our teacher was becoming extremely impatient with us. When we all filed into the classroom, the teacher began to raise her voice, telling us to pick up our papers. I scurried to the blue bucket and grabbed only one of my two assignments, unknowingly leaving behind the second paper along with a special pencil I had borrowed from my mom. When the teacher saw there were still many papers and pencils left in the blue bucket from other students, she lost her temper. Raising the unclaimed papers in the air, she screamed, "F's! ALL F's!" and ripped them into four, jagged, uneven squares.

Ms. Klotz then picked up the borrowed pencil I accidentally left in the blue bucket and walked toward the trashcan. Suddenly realizing the forgotten pencil, I began to get up to rescue it. But I was stopped short with a hostile look and mean word from my teacher saying, "Nope." as she threw it hard in the trash can. I couldn't believe she threw my mom's special pencil away. (Because it was my mom's, I ended up rescuing it from the trash when the teacher's back was turned.) I spent hours that night sobbing from all the stress and anxiety of the whole situation.

This was not an isolated incident. Repeated incidents like the story above, on almost a daily basis, led me to believe that I was always doing something wrong—that I couldn't do anything right. My elementary school brain mistakenly concluded that if I made even the smallest mistake, I wasn't worthy to even keep my own pencil. There were many lessons I learned that I would like to have done without.

My grasp on whatever peace and happiness I had that year was easily lost, but not so easily replaced. The negative environment of the classroom began to have a devastating effect on my confidence.

I felt terrible...inside and outside of class. My neck would burn red-hot and my stomach would churn with nausea before I walked in the classroom. I was afraid to ask questions, but felt the need to ask more questions about every single thing because I was afraid of messing up a small detail and being criticized. I felt like it seemed I couldn't do anything right. A running dialogue of "I'm always doing something wrong" began running though my mind. I began to constantly say "I'm sorry" after any thing that I did or said that wasn't "perfect."

Overall, I grew afraid of people of all ages. I felt ashamed and that I did not belong and had no right at all to speak, make an impact, or influence my surrounding environment and world.

The distortions I let myself believe led to months of stress, pain and regular emotional breakdowns. About half way through the year, when I was on the verge of another tearful episode, my mom gave me some priceless advice...

"Every problem can work for your good."

I paused as I thought about it. Stepping back from the midst of the struggle, I realized that I could look at the situation from another point of view where there were no overwhelming emotions to get in the way of clear thinking.

I thought, what was the good that could come from my challenging situation?

I realized that I had the opportunity to make myself grow. I realized that I could decide to use this challenge to make me stronger—to build myself up. I could actually use the struggle up this mountain in my life to help me reach the top stronger, braver, and more confident than ever.

To do this, I realized that my first step up to the summit was that I had to separate myself from my teacher's negative comments and mean remarks that kept dragging me down to the bottom.

Instead of focusing on how bad my teacher made me feel, I decided to look and see how I could tackle that mountain of self doubt and raise my confidence regardless of what she said.

I realized that who I am as a wonderful person is independent of her opinion—and of anyone's opinion, really. I decided to

173

break free of trying to live up to someone else's unhealthy standards and expectations. With each choice, with each conscious decision to see the situation differently, I took one more step up on my climb.

It was a long journey, but as the years passed, I found that as I stretched myself to remain calm despite the criticisms of others, I could begin to discern what was truth and what was a lie. My quiet statement of "I'm sorry" that had been sprinkled through everything I used to say, began to be replaced with confident smiles, opinions, and ideas. My slumped shoulders were replaced by a great posture and my head held high!

I realized that I could apply this "everything happens for good" approach to any situation, any place, or any other "mountain" in my life! This realization has served me well through the years. For example, at the beginning of my junior year of high school, because I was interested in the idea of court and law, I tried out for my school's "Mock Trial Team" where you get to experience what it is like to be a lawyer. Two of my closest friends were going out for the team as well. It was only a few days later when the results were posted: both of my friends had made the team, and I had not. I was pretty bummed out! But I knew that I couldn't focus all of my time on how disappointed I felt, wishing for a different outcome. "Everything happens for good," I repeated to myself.

I applied the lesson that I had learned so many years ago in elementary school: What was the good in this situation?

Instead of focusing on what I was going to miss out on and why I didn't get in, I decided to look at how I could use the time I would have spent on the Mock Trial Team on something better.

I focused on my other passions. I believe that everyone, including young people, have a lot of wisdom to share and I wanted to help other students realize "the good" in life and to find their confidence, despite tough situations.

I decided to use the time I would have spent on the "mock trial" to actually write my own book! Because I looked at the difficult situation through a lens of possibility, I am grateful to say that I am now the nationally published author of *Wisdom without the Wrinkles, A Teen's Insights on How to Be A Successful Leader, Earn Respect and Create an Amazing Life*, that I authored at the age of just 16!

Because I approached the situation with a positive attitude, looking for the good in it, the result was a happy, more contented me — and a nationally published book that is helping teens nation-wide! I even had additional time for extra-curricular activities, including a cooking class with a famous chef!

That special lesson I learned in elementary school — to look for the good that could come from a problem — helped me to realize that I had the power to override someone else's negative influence. When faced with a situation, I ultimately get to choose what I feel! So do you!

The mental strength we have inside of us is one of the greatest forces we possess! We are influenced by our interpretation of what we hear. When we take in information, we process it and repeat it to ourselves. If other people, who cannot actually be inside our heads, can have so much influence, imagine the positive possibilities we could have if we regularly told ourselves encouraging, constructive things. Imagine what would happen if we took our difficult circumstances and looked at them differently—through the lens of possibility and opportunity?

You have the power to make the most of whatever life throws at you! The way you approach things determines your mood and your actions. Find ways to remind yourself to see the good that can come from difficult situations. Always look for windows and doors of possibilities, not the walls!

How?

Ask yourself:

- "How can this problem work for my good?"
- "How can I make the most of this challenging situation?"
- Who is one trusted person or friend that can help me with this challenge?

- "When I overcome this challenge, what positive skill, ability or character trait will I have developed or strengthened that I can be proud of?"

Today, I can actually look back and even feel grateful for my year with "Ms. Klotz" because I learned much more than just reading and math. I learned the priceless lesson that every problem can work for good. This began the journey to conquer my mountain of self-doubt where I found my confidence at the summit!

The same is true for you! Whatever mountain you face — a difficulty, a tough time, a challenging situation — you have the ability to overcome it!

Remember, "Every problem can work for your good," and this can make all the difference in your life! So keep climbing — it's a great view at the top!

You Are Worth It!

— By —
Devony Miller

On the very first day of high school, I took nervous steps to my first class. I couldn't believe that I was finally here – high school!

I was so self-conscious, though! I felt overwhelmed by all the unfamiliar faces, and the critical eyes of the upperclassmen seemed to be judging every person that walked by – including me.

Of course, while many were friendly, many seemed to whisper to each other and gossip about me and my fellow first-year students. It was extremely intimidating, and at that point, I was not feeling particularly optimistic about my freshman year.

The especially mysterious part about high school was all these guys I'd never seen before. I thought that as a freshman I would be invisible, but immediately I found that I was very wrong. I had classes that had upperclassmen in them, and I found many of them hopelessly flirting with me. Honestly, at first, it felt great to have all that attention. I felt flattered and it made me feel pretty and wanted. In fact, there was one particular upperclassman that had noticed me. He was really smooth about approaching me, and he made it very difficult to determine if he liked me or not. But through the long lines of rumors, I learned that this guy had a particular interest for me. I really liked him, too!

My parents were concerned as they learned more about the guy. They were worried about our difference in age—I was just fourteen and the youngest person in the entire high school. He was seventeen. Because I had always been responsible and strong in my values and boundaries, my parents nervously trusted I could handle the relationship.

As the time flew by, and we spent more time together, the guy and I began a dating relationship rather quickly. I remember the day it happened. He called me one afternoon after I got home from my cross country practice, and he asked me if he could consider me his girlfriend. I was blushing at the other end of the receiver, and shyly, I said yes. My heart fluttered. It was the start of something that seemed wonderful.

For a while, everything was wonderful. While he called me only a few times a week, we were always communicating. Even though we were both really involved in sports, we always found time for each other. We would consider it odd to go a day without at least some form of conversation. As we spent more time together and learned more about each other, our relationship intensified on an emotional level.

At the time, I felt so glad to have him. He seemed sweet and thoughtful. He would go out of his way for me and surprise me with gifts. I was falling for him, and on the night of the homecoming dance, he told me he loved me for the first time. I felt that he meant it with all his heart, and I trusted every word of it. How could he not?

We were happy, and everything was going well for me. I was an athlete, I was getting all As, and I had an exciting life. Even though I was just a freshman, my choices to stand out in a good way were set, as I had big goals and tried to do my best and be my best.

Many would say that he did not have as much going for him. For starters, he did not have favorable grades or really care about them. In fact, we were in the same Spanish class, and I helped tutor him so he could pass. He also didn't really seem to have any real aspirations or goals, and some of his choices were questionable. Plus he wasn't very supportive of my choices — more on that later.

Even though a lot of "little red flags" kept popping up as we were dating, I wanted to look past my concerns — and be the best girlfriend I could and try to appreciate his heart.

That is why I was surprised that he stopped treating me well. Only two months into our relationship, and the disrespect started to grow. I didn't understand what was happening and thought maybe I had done something wrong. For example, one time I got sick for a couple of days; I felt terrible with a fever and a chronic headache, which almost made it impossible to move. Of course, my boyfriend would be worried! Right? I kept crawling over to my phone to check my messages to see if he had tried to contact me. Nope. Nothing.

Being sick was awful, and the constant flow of get-better wishes from my friends was a relief; however, he didn't reach out to me — not once! I was so upset that he made no attempt to even see if I was OK. He didn't even check on me once.

As the days went on, excuses raced through my mind as I tried not to doubt him. I thought of coincidences like maybe he was sick, too, or maybe he had a family emergency. Those were the only explanations I could think of, and they didn't seem very likely. As I got well enough, my heart was in knots, as I decided to confront him.

After I returned back to school, I asked why he didn't check in to see if I was OK. He commented in a rude tone that he did not *have* to.

I felt myself grow smaller as he said those words to me. My heart broke, and it hurt even worse to know he did not care. But, trying to make excuses, I told myself to ignore it because it was "not a big deal." But, <u>it was</u>. By making excuses and overlooking his disrespect, I was letting him step on me instead of standing up for myself—and was slowly losing myself in the process.

He continued to be rude to me, disrespect me, neglect me, and ignore me. I no longer felt special—I felt the opposite. He thought by doing this he could control me and manipulate me, and he was right—up to a point. There were just certain things I would not compromise on—more on that later. I went out of my way for him, I sacrificed for him, and I received nothing in return. I would try so hard for a moment of his attention. It was exhausting.

The disrespect continued—even when I was honored, along with the rest of the varsity cross country girls, for qualifying to the Cross Country State Championships (which is a big deal—especially for me being a freshman). The entire school even had a pep rally for us! All the teachers, the staff, my friends, and my family were there to celebrate and pump us up for the big race. Afterwards, all the students and teachers lined up to congratulate us face-to-face. Even better, all the students that stayed did not have to go back to class. This is how I knew my boyfriend must be in line to congratulate me—he was always looking for an opportunity to miss class, and, of course, he would want to take a moment to congratulate me! Right? I could not wait to see him!

Well, one-by-one the students went by, and he did not show. I could not understand. There were friends, acquaintances, and even strangers that stood in line to congratulate me, but my own boyfriend did not even look at me before we left for the state meet.

Meanwhile, I kept ignoring all those red flags—and they were getting bigger and bigger by the day. In a moment of hopelessness, I even confronted him and asked him if he still wanted to be with me. This woke him up, and he started being sweet again, like before. That good time was short lived; he proved me wrong once again, and things got even worse—that's when the pressure began.

Looking back, the biggest red flag of all during this time was that he began strongly pressuring me physically and trying to disrespect my own personal boundaries.

As an athlete and a leader, I've always tried to make the best choices for me—to avoid the distractions of alcohol, tobacco, and other drugs and other situations that may be dangerous or harmful. I also made the decision to resist the tremendous pressures to "get physical" in relationships or hook up. I set my boundaries high and made my choice clear. For me, I knew that my personal choice to wait was the best way for me to stay focused on my goals, protect my heart, and respect my body as well as avoid some pretty heavy duty consequences—both emotional and physical—that I saw were hurting a lot of my friends.

As I continued to stay true to myself, my positive decisions and my personal boundaries, I saw very quickly that it is possible to have fun, be liked, and have amazing friendships and crazy-good times. In fact, it was because of those positive choices that I was able to have an even better and more successful life—including incredible friendships and great times—without all the risks and consequences. (I am proud to be completely drug-free and alcohol-free as I write this as a senior in high school.)

While the pressures on me to use alcohol and other drugs were small in comparison, when it came to dating and relationships, the pressure of getting physical was overwhelming. I wasn't the only one—I even witnessed others being bullied or harassed for their personal choices, high standards, and strong boundaries.

While most respected me for my choice, some made fun of me and others gossiped about me, but what hurt worst of all, was when my boyfriend started seriously pressuring me—even though he knew of my choice to wait. This hurt me because I was comfortable with my boundaries, and I didn't want to change them.

The pressure began when he started inferring that he wanted more. He started trying to convince me that it was okay and was not a "big deal". He said that if I really loved him, I would give him what he wanted.

This pressure happened again and again. I did my best to be true to myself and my personal choice and told him no. I'll be honest — it was difficult to be strong and stand-up for what I believe in, but I knew deep down that if he really loved me, he would not pressure me. I knew if he really loved me, he would respect and support my personal decision. I tucked these thoughts away as I hoped, time and again, that he would change and grow to accept and love me for me.

But, he kept on trying. He did not stop. He made me believe that my personal boundaries and my choice didn't matter and that "because he was a guy" that it was okay for my boyfriend to pressure me. I don't care who someone is, you and your personal boundaries deserve to be respected.

Day after day passed, and the pressure continued, and I continued to try to stay true to myself. After a while, it became very clear to him that he would not achieve his ultimate goal. In December of my freshman year, he called me for the last time. He said he was breaking up with me. I was so upset. The feeling of hopelessness was overwhelming for me.

For a long time, I felt like I was being punished for my choice and would never find someone else. In reality, though, it was my personal choice that protected me.

Even if I had gone against my standards and had "given him what he wanted," the truth is that our relationship would have ended anyway. Why? Healthy and lasting relationships are built on genuine love and respect for a person—not bullying or pressuring someone to compromise themselves or their personal boundaries. Even if he had gotten "what he wanted," he would have most likely broken up with me anyway, like he already had done with so many other girls.

What all the hardships and heartbreak of that unhealthy dating relationship taught me is that <u>no one</u> is worth compromising your standards, personal boundaries and values! You deserve respect, and you need to stay true to yourself.

After ending that unhealthy relationship I realized that I needed to set higher standards for future dating relationships. This is what opened the door to something wonderful. Looking back, I'm actually so happy the other guy broke up with me!

Why? Because as I continued to keep my personal boundaries and focus on my goals, I developed an amazing year-long friendship with a wonderful young man who truly loves and accepts me for me. Because we were friends for so long, I really got to know him and his heart. He became my best friend. (By the way, friends first is a great way to start any dating relationship!) After over a year of being friends, we started dating!

Being in this new relationship—dating my best friend—I got to see what a healthy relationship is really all about! We bring out the best in each other, we support one another, and he loves me for me. He 100 percent respects me, my choice, and my personal boundaries, too!

In dating him, I've come to realize that the best relationships are those based on a foundation of friendship, loyalty, love, trust, and RESPECT.

I want you to know that there is never ever any excuse, ever, for someone to disrespect you, your choices, or your physical boundaries. Never let someone justify pressuring you, because it will never be okay under any circumstances.

If someone says "Hey, if you loved me, you would do it," then you need to respond with "Hey, if you really loved me, you wouldn't pressure me to."

This also means paying close attention to the red flags of an unhealthy relationship, such as yelling, lying, pressuring, name calling, physical or emotional abuse, and controlling. The second they happen in a relationship—NO excuses! Any disrespect of any kind in a relationship is a BIG RED FLAG. It is a warning that needs to be taken seriously rather than turned into self-blame or an excuse for continued bad behavior!

It's about reminding yourself that because you deserve better, you deserve to move on from that unhealthy relationship—NOW.

If you are the victim of dating violence or abuse—please know this is not your fault! Tell a trusted adult or counselor right away. You deserve support to rebuild your heart and take back your life.

If you've been pressured and made choices you regret, you are not alone. Please know that because each day is a new day, you can make a new and different choice from this day forward. It's your body and your life! Think about what your own personal boundaries and standards are. Rather than compromise, stay true to yourself—and require respect.

While it may seem flattering for an older guy or someone who is popular to like you, be careful. Take the time to find someone who is a person of character and integrity, who respects you and your personal boundaries, and who supports your own goals and dreams.

There are wonderful guys out there that are cute and respectful, just as there are some that are rude and obnoxious. You just have to find the right type of person, and that person is out there. Don't ever lower your standards or compromise your personal boundaries for someone, because there is someone else out there that is perfect for you and will respect you for you. Also remember it is awesome to be single, too.

It's okay for you to choose to wait to date or not be in a romantic relationship. A relationship — if it is positive — should complement you and your life, not detract from it!

You deserve love and you deserve to be treated right. Most importantly, you deserve respect.

Why?

Because, you are worth it!

Psst...You Are Not Alone!

By
Nicole Thor

The August before I started college as a recent high school grad, I went on a trip to a big city with twenty-five other incoming freshmen. We spent a week there doing service projects like cleaning up a park and helping out at a retirement home. When we weren't doing community service, we stayed at a hostel (it's like a house combined with a hotel), and all twenty girls slept in one giant bedroom.

One evening, we had had a long day of community service. I was exhausted and just wanted to go to sleep. I was lying on my thin mattress with my sheet over my head, hoping to block out some of the light from the room and the noise from the other girls. Once in a while I would look up during a particularly interesting comment. I couldn't believe that they weren't tired at all.

A few of the girls had been planning an "intervention" for a couple of days. As soon as Beth found out that Amy had never been to a college party, she told all the other girls, and they decided to spend one night telling Amy "everything she needs to know before starting college." I knew immediately that this "intervention" was a bad idea.

That night, the very first question Beth asked Amy made her blush—and that was only the beginning. From that point on, a large number of the girls began to surround Amy—but not all of them. I was not the only one staying out of this. A few of the girls began to describe in vivid detail the different methods, processes, and tactics of various aspects of "the college lifestyle" that were *far* from positive. Amy's confusion and concern were clearly visible as it was with some of the other girls, too. Many of the girls in the circle were quiet as they nervously looked at the few girls who were doing most of the talking.

As the talk continued, I felt more and more disgusted by the things that the group leaders said. They were making it out to be that "EVERYONE" was doing these things and they were a REQUIRED part of college. At that point, I got so frustrated that I gave up trying to sleep at all because it was clear that it wouldn't happen — not with all that crazy nonsense being said.

I sat up in bed and saw two other girls across the room, Cassie and Daisy, who were outside the group but were wide awake and listening in as well. Their reactions to these comments made it clear that they were feeling exactly the same as I was. After impressive but relatively ineffective faux sign language, we decided it would be much easier to text each other.

"this is ridiculous…amy does not need to hear any of this. look at her face…she's scared out of her mind"

"i know!!! they're just using this time to talk about their 'experiences.' they're not actually trying to help her"

"the worst part is that amy is going to think that this is the only way to live…because even though it's just a few girls talking, they are all saying the exact same thing in the middle of this huge group!"

"SERIOUSLY!!!!! what they are saying is not true at all!"

Eventually I decided it would be even easier to join them on the other side of the room, so I grabbed my blanket and climbed up to the bunk they were sitting on. From this new vantage point, I could see that other girls in the room were also sitting up, listening, shaking their heads, and rolling their eyes at the ridiculousness of the "advice" they, too, heard Beth and a few other girls telling Amy.

We whispered to each other in hushed tones on how inappropriate, inaccurate, and even dangerous the messages were for Amy—or anyone.

Concerned, I said, "This is going to scar her for life, especially if she feels forced into doing these things. When this is over, we need to pull her aside and tell her the truth."

After a while, the girl "spokespersons" who had staged the intervention, decided that it was getting late and they had covered enough for the night. As the big group split up and the girls walked to their separate bunks, the spokespersons were loudly proclaiming how awesome the talk was—and some of the other girls awkwardly acted like they agreed.

As Amy slipped out of the room to head down to the kitchen for a snack, Cassie, Daisy, and I followed. Once downstairs, we tried to comfort her as best we could because she still looked like a deer in headlights.

"Amy, you can forget everything they just said. We know that you're not the crazy party-girl, get drunk, use drugs, and hook-up type, and you don't have to be. It's awesome to be drug-free. It's awesome to drink a soda instead of beer. It's awesome to be single and wait and if you decide to date, choose someone who loves and respects you and your choices!"

Momentum was building as another girl said, "Yeah! Just because you're going to college, does not mean you need to live like that. Actually, if you listen to them, you would think that EVERYONE in college is like that—the truth is that the majority aren't out binge drinking every weekend. There are some who do, and because they are very vocal about their choices, people think that it's *everyone*.

Gaining even more determination, I shared, "Yeah there are plenty of other people who don't party like that. I don't. My friends don't—and we have a blast!"

Another girl lowered her voice as she earnestly shared, "Most people who live that way aren't even happy; they just pretend to be because everyone else looks happy."

Another somber young woman who spoke with a deep sense of knowing said, "There are serious consequences that come with stuff like that, too; those girls talking didn't even mention those things."

As we continued to tell her how the last couple of hours were a complete lie, I could see the worry lines disappear from her face and her shaking slowly start to die down. Amy told us with relief that she would be okay, and we all headed back upstairs for bed.

As I thought about it, I was proud that Cassie, Daisy, and I had done the right thing in telling Amy the truth. I also knew that we could've done something even better. We could have stopped the "intervention" as soon as we heard where it was headed. This would've saved Amy from hearing all of the lies in the first place.

As I reflected on the situation and my own life as a student, I drew strength from the fact that there were many of us in the room who disagreed with the destructive messages in the "intervention." I was curious how many of the girls would have actually sided with us instead, if Cassie, Daisy, and I had stepped up in the first place. Based upon what I know now, I'm sure at least half of them would have, or at least the others may have been less persistent with their negative comments and influence.

Think about it. If you hear two groups shouting in another room and the smaller group is shouting louder than the larger group, the smaller group is going to sound bigger than it is. Right?

This can be the same in real life — but can actually be dangerous. Here's why. We live in a world where television, movies, music videos, on-line messages, and even our groups of friends can give us a lot of "noise" about how alcohol, drugs, and hooking up is what is popular or expected. Even though, according to my own experience and also a lot of research, the majority of students are actually making many good choices, you'd never know it. No wonder so many students who are trying to stay on the best path and make the best choices, feel alone. Not only that, but sadly, some are also pressured into living according to the "hype" because they think everyone else is — instead of choosing what is ultimately best for them and their future.

What's even worse is that while all the noise about these destructive behaviors gets a lot of attention, the real and serious consequences that come with these choices don't.

If you have felt pressured into making choices that don't serve you or your future, I don't think it's your fault. You may have been lied to by all the "noise," but you can always choose to get your life back on track. It starts with your choice! Even finding just one friend or mentor who supports or encourages you and your positive choices can be a huge help!

If you are already trying to make the best choices for you — be strong! When you are surrounded by all the noise shouting lies at you, and you feel like you're alone, do yourself a favor! Speak up and remember that you are actually part of a positive-choice majority! Host your own intervention! Talk with your friends, be more vocal about your choices, be proud of the great decisions you are making and stay strong in the face of peer pressure.

Most importantly, remember that far more powerful than words, your actions can speak louder than any megaphone!

Your efforts may start with a quiet whisper, but you will see — they can quickly turn into bold and confident declarations! In turn, you will inspire and help others to make great choices too!

Psst....<u>You</u> are not alone! Pass it on!

Add Faith, Trust and Pixie Dust!

By
Madeline Lanshe

"What do you want to be when you grow up?"

I'm sure you were asked this question dozens of times as a child—and I found that this doesn't stop when you become a teenager, either. Instead, it changes to "What do you want to study in college?" or "What do you want to do when you graduate college?"

Since about the age of nine, I've known the answer to this question. But it wasn't until recently, at age nineteen, that I've been brave enough to answer it out loud with confidence.

At sixteen, I got a cellphone, bought a car, and started college all in one month. (I started college early!) Prior to that was my graduation party. You can probably guess the most asked question of the day. It was something along the lines of "What do you want to do with your life?" Yikes! What a scary question. Luckily, I knew.

Unfortunately, I'd been conditioned not to tell the truth. Why? When I was asked about what I wanted to do with my life, there was a brief period of time when I did tell the truth and the conversations would go something like this:

"I want to write," I'd say.

"What kind of stuff do you want to write?" they would ask.

"Fiction novels. Fantasy, to be more specific," I'd share with excitement.

At age eight or nine, people think it's cute. But at sixteen, it's a different story. Usually, I was met with a blank stare.

I would wonder, What did I say? Do I have something in my teeth?

Then, after the blank stare would be a confused "Oh?" And finally, the soul-crushing follow-up remark, "If you like to write, you could go into journalism or something."

Cue the cricket sounds. I must have missed the connection. What does journalism and reporting on news have to do with writing fantasy novels? That's like saying, "Oh, you want to be an engineer and help build bridges? Since you like math, maybe you should be a math teacher instead." There's nothing wrong with either of those occupations, but if your passion is engineering and building things, teaching isn't going to cut it for most people. The reverse is also true. Just because math is involved in both doesn't mean they are even close to being the same career.

So, the "crickets" would continue "chirping" because what do you say in return to that?

How about this? (Insert sarcasm here.) "I never thought of journalism and writing news articles! It is completely the same as writing a fantasy novel with characters from another world. What life-changing advice!"

The last sentence, at least, is true. For me, these responses from strangers and relatives did change my life, just not in the good way they probably hoped.

I was met with similar reactions nearly every time I told someone my dream. These adults, much older and more experienced, looked at me like I was a strange character from a foreign land — like in one of the fantasy novels I was writing. It was really embarrassing and made me feel like my dream was childish and silly.

There were some people who would say an uncertain, "That's cool." But it was obvious that they were merely humoring me. They didn't take me or my dream seriously. They thought that I was young and that once I was in the "real world," I'd be realistic.

I don't think these adults were trying to lower my spirits or embarrass me. I think they thought it was their duty to make me realize just how difficult my dream was. They sincerely felt the need to remind me that there are thousands of manuscripts and authors that never, ever get published and to explain how challenging the publishing process is. They spoke like experts about my odds, even though I'm sure I've done more research on the subject than they have.

"Besides," they'd continue, "do you know how many people make their living by writing novels? You could always write in your spare time." Frustrated, I'd imagine saying back to them, "No, I don't know that number. Do you? And what does it have to do with me?"

I continued to let these things get deep under my skin, and by the time it was my high school graduation party, I was already prepared with an alternative answer — "I don't know what I want to do yet."

After sharing my rehearsed answer, there would be smiles and a reassuring, "That's okay, you have lots of time," or a good-natured, "You'd better figure it out!"

The truth is I much preferred these types of comments to the other responses, which seemed to directly attack my dream.

It's funny, looking back at it all now, because if my passion was leading me to become a doctor, I'm sure neither I nor anyone else would be questioning it.

Since being a writer of fiction novels isn't a typical nine-to-five or "stable" job, the blank stares and discouraging remarks, unfortunately, had burrowed deep into my head.

This paired with some of my insecurities about writing added up to some major self-doubt. After all, at the time of graduation, I hadn't shared my writing with anyone and wouldn't do so until my junior year in college. Even though I loved to write, how did I know that it was what I was supposed to be doing? And wasn't saying that I wanted to be a writer kind of arrogant? Who was I to say my writing would ever be that good?

It wasn't until the beginning of January that my attitude and life started to change.

My oldest brother introduced me to this speaker and author, Julie Carrier, and her BeYOUtiful® Club. I learned that it is a positive role model and leadership club for extraordinary girls and young women who care about setting big goals, being their best, and inspiring others to do the same.

I was excited but also very nervous. I usually shy away from new experiences, for fear of the unknown. But I decided to go way out of my comfort zone to become a part of this once-in-a-lifetime opportunity.

A big part of the BeYOUtiful® Club is all about mentoring. During a mentoring conversation, Julie asked me about my life and my dreams. I told her I was majoring in French, which I chose for the simple fact that I like the language and had planned on continuing to study it regardless. She asked me what I wanted to do with that degree.

But I already knew I didn't want to do anything with it. I was tempted to just say my usual — tell her I didn't really know what I wanted to do yet. But what was the point in that? If I was going to get anything out of the experience, I had to be honest and take a positive risk.

So I told her about my passion for writing. I probably held my breath as I waited for her to say something. Would she think I was childish, too? Her not only enthusiastic but also interested response took me by surprise. I cringe when I think of what could have happened if I'd told her something different. Our monthly get-togethers and activities might have been centered on French instead of my love of fiction writing. Little by little my confidence in my dream grew as did my confidence that writing was the path I was supposed to follow.

But it really hit me when I was invited by Julie to go to one of the most magical places on Earth, no less — the place where dreams come true (and there is a big castle right in the middle to prove it) — to attend her BeYOUtiful® Dream It to Be It leadership weekend! You know where I'm talking about, right? Just think, "mouse ears!"

At the leadership weekend, I finally got to meet Julie face to face, as well as many of the other girls in the group from all over the country. We spent the weekend doing exciting exercises to build our confidence and to help make road maps for our futures. The other girls had amazing dreams, too, and they could relate to what I had been going through.

For one of the exercises, we each had a blank pop-up cardboard silhouette of a person that represented who we were on the inside. With brightly colored markers, we wrote all of the things that we know for sure on the head, the positive traits or talents we have in the middle, and the lessons we've learned from the past on the right leg. The left leg would remain blank until the following day.

Later was our "Dream It to Be It" dinner at one of the most beautiful restaurants ever overlooking the castle! This wasn't just any dinner — it was a celebration of ourselves — *ten years into the future!*

We had to pretend, as soon as we stepped into the restaurant, that it was our ten-year reunion and we had already accomplished our dreams. So right when we walked through the doors, we started squealing and hugging and saying how much we missed each other and how we couldn't believe it had been ten years already.

I'm about as far from an actress as they come, so I knew this exercise was going to be very difficult and uncomfortable.

But, just like the first time I talked with Julie, I decided to jump in with both feet.

As we sat and waited for our food in the gorgeous restaurant, we asked each other what had happened since the last time we saw one another "ten years ago."

We had all been asked to bring some sort of a prop or visual, too, so earlier that day I made a book cover and taped it over my journal. It read Bestselling Author along with my book title, name, and a testimonial from my favorite author. I presented it at the table and said it was my third book to be published and the first of a trilogy. I smiled as I talked about how a movie was even in the works and I was helping with the casting process. Julie, the other girls, and my mom asked me questions and presented their props, and we supported and celebrated each other.

Soon, it didn't feel like we were pretending at all, and it became easier and easier. It was incredible to be surrounded by other people who supported my dream and by other girls who had big dreams, too. There was absolutely no judgment in our group, and even though we were in the middle of a very public restaurant, I wasn't embarrassed. I was confident. Before, I'd been reluctant to even tell my dream. But at that point, I was acting it out in public with no fear.

The longer we conversed and the more I shared about my career as an author of fiction, the more I knew that this was what I was supposed to be doing and what I wanted. I finally realized that it didn't matter what everyone else thought or said. This was my path — and my dream.

Because we were having so much fun, we played this game for about two and a half hours — which Julie said was the record. After dinner we put on our mouse ears and watched twinkling fireworks on the balcony of the restaurant overlooking the beautiful castle. I couldn't have asked for a more magical and special moment in a place that exists only because of a remarkable visionary's own unique dream (that started with just a mouse) so many years ago. I felt so happy — like I could fly!

While I was shining with confidence on the outside, my biggest success from the experience was something internal. It was by "dreaming it to be it" that I finally knew and accepted that I am meant to be a writer.

The day after the dinner, we had to write our dream for the future on the left leg of the cardboard silhouette, which symbolized ourselves in the future. With confidence and a new sense of peace, I wrote, "I am a writer."

A smile spread across my face as I realized that it was no longer something that I hoped might happen. It became something I know I am meant to do, and something I am going to do.

I'm no longer embarrassed by my dream. I don't freak out anymore trying to figure out what I'm going to do. I used to lose so many hours of sleep and peace worrying about my future. No more.

Now, I am much bolder in sharing my choice to be a writer.

Have the remarks and responses from others changed? No, but the way I handle them has. I listen patiently as people tell me I could just work for a publishing company or be a journalist. They don't understand my dream, and that's okay. I don't need them to anymore. There are some times when I still hesitate. There is still a temptation to merely say "I don't know what I want to do with my life," but now I know I don't have to pour my heart out to people who don't understand. What I do have to do is honor my dream and myself by at least telling the truth.

Encouraged by the support of the other girls in Florida, I made the choice to share with them some of my fiction writing for a book I am working on. Outside of my writing classes, this is something I'd never done before. It's hard sharing something so personal, but I couldn't ask for more supportive people.

Because taking action turns dreams into reality, I also set aside time to write more, signed up for more creative writing classes, and declared writing as my minor.

I'll be graduating soon with a major in French and a minor in creative writing. I'm even considering going on to obtain a master's in creative writing. I know I might have to work a second job before I can actually make a living solely by writing, but because being a full-time author is my ultimate goal, I will work harder than hard to reach it.

Maybe you, too, have a dream that isn't typical or common. If so, then you may have similar doubts and obstacles in your way or may face them as you get older.

Maybe you want to be a scientist, an actress, a singer. Maybe you want to start your own business and be the CEO. Whatever it is, I beg you to not give it up or be pressured into doing something "practical" or "typical" or that you have no passion for. I've witnessed many people give up on their dreams for something they don't really want to do, and, ultimately, it doesn't make them happy. It's a tragedy. Don't let others make you feel embarrassed by your dream and make you feel that you aren't good enough or it isn't possible. Because the truth is, they don't have a clue. You are the only one who truly knows yourself and what you are capable of. You are capable of great things, unique things, and big dreams!

Not everyone is going to understand your dream, but it is really important to find one or two people who are supportive—who you can talk to and cry to when things get rough.

The only way this is possible is if you take the risk of sharing your dream with people. It's worth all the negative remarks if you find even just one supportive person. Without someone reminding you that you can do it and should do it, it is much easier to give up and settle for doing something you don't love.

Maybe you can't go to Julie's BeYOUtiful® Dream It to Be It event (or even if you can), be willing to embrace your dream and take positive chances. This means going out of your comfort zone and diving into the unknown, which can be the hardest and scariest thing to do. But I know, for myself, regret is one of the worst feelings ever. The last thing I want to do is surrender my dream and be plagued with the question of "what if?" when I'm older.

As I reflect on my magical time at Julie's Dream It to Be It weekend where I felt my dreams take flight, I realize that helping your big goals and dreams get off the ground takes three things: faith, trust, and dash of pixie dust!

Faith. Remember when you were a child and nothing seemed impossible or out of reach? Recapture that mindset! You need to have faith in yourself and your goals to help them fly. You can't know for certain that you won't fall or stumble as you try—that is why it is called faith. The more you try, the more you learn. The more you learn, the more you succeed!

Trust. You need to trust in yourself and your abilities. You need to trust that you have your talents and passions for a reason, and you are meant to pursue them. You need to trust that you are here for a purpose that is yours to fulfill. Find at least one person who trusts and believes in you and helps you believe and trust in yourself.

Pixie Dust. And, of course, you need an element of magic to fly. I like to think of it as passion. Passion is what makes the ordinary, extraordinary and turns the regular dust into something magical. Passion is the spark that lights up when you are working on something you truly love!

As we get older, it becomes harder to have faith and to trust in ourselves. The "real world" makes sure of that.

The good news is that most of us already have "pixie dust"—and I'm not really talking about the magical glitter-like golden powder you may see in movies that grants the abilities of flight. I'm talking about those things you are passionate about—the things that add a twinkle to your eye and make your heart soar.

Sadly, so many people often ignore these things or forget they have them. But your passions are too precious and magical to let them go to waste. Think about what you are passionate about! Make those things a part of your life!

Then, the next time you are asked, "What do you want to be when you grow up?" remember to add some faith, trust, and pixie dust! With it, you will soar, as your dreams take flight!

Wear Your "Fuzzy Boots!"

_____ *By* _____
Julia Scappatura

"I want to be a pop star!"

Well, that is something I'd say in fourth grade, that is. I had everything from unique clothes to trendy hair and felt I was well on my way.

I liked the idea of having my own style that was different from everyone else—and I just knew that to be a pop star, the right pair of shoes would make the whole outfit! For my unique pop star style, I had this vision of no ordinary shoes, however—I knew that they had to be fuzzy boots!

Of course, the boots were difficult to find. So, when I took up the task, actually, it became more of a mission! There was no stopping me! These were not ordinary fuzzy boots I was looking for, either. They needed to be the ultimate one-of-a-kind pair of fuzzy boots—just the right amount of fluffiness, fuzziness, and awesomeness!

My parents took me to every store in town with no luck. As a last resort, we went to an old shoe warehouse where the kind of shoes nobody wants anymore go to grow old. I was about to give up. Then, tucked away in the back corner, between a pair of pink and white sneakers and black dress shoes with huge silver buckles on them, I saw the most glorious sight! It was like there was a beam of light shining on them from the sky! There were the fuzziest pair of fuzzy boots I had ever seen!

I was so excited that I flung off my worn-out orange and purple shoes and placed my feet into the beautiful boots in front of me. I was so happy that I started to sing and perform a fun pop song, right there in the corner of the warehouse. My happiness was short-lived, though, when I quickly realized that the boots were too big for me. I ran around the store frantically looking for a smaller pair, but there were none to be found.

I decided I would just have to keep them and come up with a creative way to make them fit. After trial and error, I found the best method was to stuff the toes of each boot. That weekend, I practiced how to walk in the boots without falling. I loved those boots!

Monday morning, I sprung out of bed and got dressed for school. I put on my favorite outfit and did my hair perfectly. I ran downstairs, ate my breakfast and had all my things packed. Now was the moment — the final touch to the outfit — I put on my big fuzzy boots and a big smile on my face. I knew that this was going to be a perfect day!

I made it to class and was totally prepared to show off my new boots during recess! In class I eagerly was waiting for the bell to ring so I could run outside to show all my friends. During class, though, I kept hearing giggles and whispers behind me. I turned around and saw a group of girls pointing and looking at my boots. I smiled as I thought to myself "They must think that my boots are pretty awesome."

Little did I know what they were really thinking, but I soon learned the truth. After class was over, I went out into the hallway and I heard my name mentioned and saw a group of kids laughing and talking. I wandered a little closer to hear them better. One boy said, "Did you see Julia... wow, <u>what</u> is she wearing? Those boots are so ugly — almost as ugly as her face." Then one of the girls said, "She is so weird, who would ever wear those things? They look like she is wearing dead dogs on her feet. What a freak!" They continued to make fun of me until the teacher asked everyone to go outside for recess. As I walked outside, I was in shock, I couldn't even breathe. All I wanted to do was disappear and cry.

One of the girls walked past me and looked at my boots as she said, "Hey, Julia, I really like your boots." Then she looked at her friends and started laughing even more as she walked away.

I had never been treated like that before. I was so crushed that I started to run home. Bawling my eyes out, I tripped over my boots two or three times, but I just kept getting up and running. I knew that I needed to get as far away from those girls as fast as I could. I wanted to get home where I could feel safe.

Thankfully my home was not that far away. Both my parents worked from home and my grandparents lived with us, but they had no idea that I was going to come flying through the doorway wailing my face off. Crying hysterically, I came through the door and threw off my boots. After I had calmed down, I began to sob through the story about what had happened. When I was finished, my mother hugged me. Then she walked over and picked up the boots. I took one look and cried, "I am <u>never</u> going to wear those boots again!"

My mom replied "Oh, yes, you will. Julia, you worked so hard to find those boots and were so happy when you first put on the boots. You loved the way they looked with your outfit. Just because a group of kids at school said some mean things, you're going to stop wearing them? I love your unique style and you should never let someone take that away from you. You should wear those boots proudly!"

Feeling a little better, I told my parents that I would wear the boots in the house like slippers, but never again outside.

That didn't go over too well with my mom. She looked me right in the eyes and said "You are going right back to school, right now, with those boots on your feet."

I was horrified. I exclaimed, "No way am I going back there with those boots on..."

My mom interrupted me and told me that I would have to wear those boots once a week for the next two months. She explained that if I stopped wearing them, I was allowing the bullies to take over my life, controlling my thoughts and feelings. She helped me understand that by wearing the boots that I could stand up to the bullies and let them know I didn't care what they thought.

"Don't let the bullies win, Julia. Put your fuzzy boots back on," she said.

I knew what my mom was saying was the right thing to do, but I was still freaking out. I was imagining all the horrible things those kids were going to say when I went back to school.

I reluctantly put the boots back on and slowly walked back to school. Funny enough, it was still recess — it was as if I never

217

left. The bell rang and I walked into the school feeling like I was going to throw up. The rest of the day seemed to drag on forever. The kids wouldn't let up, but I stayed strong, remembering what my mom told me.

I was happy to hear the final bell letting me know it was time to go home. The next couple of weeks were hard. I first dreaded the time that I had to wear the boots, but over time, I became more and more confident wearing them and those students began to leave me alone.

I even started getting genuine compliments from other students and even some teachers and parents about them. Every so often, one of those bullies would make a mean comment, but it no longer bothered me as much. It's as if I had created an invisible shield and it just bounced right off. At this point, I was so proud to wear those fuzzy boots, no one was able to change my mind.

After two months, I actually became bored with wearing those boots and wanted to showcase a new style. So I retired those boots, trading them in for a new pair of shoes that matched my updated funky style.

I walked through the door of my classroom, confidently rocking out my new style and I was struck with a sudden realization! I saw that there were many girls, including my teacher (this is no joke) who were wearing fuzzy boots! These were the same kind of fuzzy boots that the bullies had made fun of me for wearing two months earlier — and now they were being worn as the height of fashion! I couldn't believe my eyes. Without knowing it, I was a trendsetter. As I stood there with my new funky shoes, gazing at all the fuzzy boots in the room, I realized that I like being unique.

From that day on, I more confidently embraced my goofy, offbeat characteristics, and the free-spirited personality that I expressed through my unique fashion style. Sometimes it was difficult and sometimes people still made fun of me — but I knew that they would probably be wearing the same thing in a few months.

Now, I am grateful for those fuzzy boots because I learned how to embrace myself and my uniqueness and discovered in the process that I could be whomever I wanted to be! I was a trendsetter. I was a leader. I was unique.

Maybe you don't own a pair of fuzzy boots, but I know that you do own many unique qualities and characteristics that make you, you!

Just like my fuzzy boots were what helped my outfit really stand out, your own "fuzzy boots" can be the unique qualities and talents that help you shine! Without "wearing" those special qualities, you become just like everyone else.

So what are your own "fuzzy boots" in your life? What are your unique qualities, talents, and characteristics that make you, you?

You are unique for a purpose — so wear your own "fuzzy boots" and walk proudly!

Be Part of the Girls Lead Movement and Join our Community!

Thousands of e-mails, phone calls and letters have poured in, and, hey, ladies, Julie heard you! So, what's all the true-to-you leadership buzz about?

You asked for it, and here it is! Drum Roll....The BeYOUtiful™ Club!

With all the crazy messages and negative examples out there for us girls...how about more positive ones for a change!?! Do you agree?

Every girl deserves to feel beautiful for who she is, achieve her goals and dreams, and have <u>positive</u> mentors and role models who encourage her to lead a positive and successful life! Do you agree!?!

So what's the BeYOUtiful™ Club? A mentoring and leadership club that helps girls maximize their full potential, build self-confidence, and develop personal success in all areas of their lives through the power of positive role models and positive messages! In short, it helps girls realize their true BeYOUty and LEAD!

What do members of the BeYOUtiful™ Club do?

- **Learn success strategies from real BeYOUty Mentors:** Girls hear from Julie and other remarkable young women all over the country who are making positive choices and have the real successes to show for it. Real models are role models!

- **Get Julie's inside scoop on inner BeYOUty tips to boost confidence, self-esteem, leadership and life skills** and how to "Be True To You!"

- **Connect with Julie and hear valuable girl guidance** on how you can live life to your full potential, too.

BeYOUtiful! It's more than just a look—it's a way to live! Join the BeYOUtiful Movement!

Want to get in the club? Check it out!

Get the rest of the BeYOUtiful™ Club Inside Scoop at...

www.BeYOUtifulClub.com

About Julie Carrier

Recognized as America's #1 Speaker for Girls

Featured on NBC's Today Show, The Education Channel and in The New York Times, Julie Carrier is recognized as "America's #1 Speaker for Girls!"

Julie has brought her message to millions of homes on national TV as an Emmy-Nominated TV Personality. Among other shows, she has been featured as a Girls' Success Coach on a positive goal setting TV show on MTV where she guides girls and young women to step out, stand up and achieve their dreams.

Seeing Julie on TV or speaking to audiences of 20-20,000, it's hard to believe her humble beginnings as an awkward middle and high school student with a growth disorder who struggled with self-doubt and being bullied. After positive role models and mentors changed her life, she

overcame the odds and experienced incredible successes at a young age, including starting her own business at the age of 14 to help pay for college.

Recognized as one of the Top 50 Student Leaders in the Nation and a Rotary International Ambassadorial Scholar to England, Julie graduated Summa Cum Laude and Phi Beta Kappa in Leadership Studies from The Ohio State University Honors Program. At the age of just 23, Julie was hired to serve as a Senior Management Consultant in Leadership Development for the Pentagon where she served for four years.

With her increasing successes, Julie became increasingly frustrated with how toxic media messages and negative role models were misleading young women away from achieving their own dreams. As a result, Julie left her prestigious Pentagon career in order to serve as a positive voice, advocate and mentor for girls on leadership, character and confidence.

Julie is the author of the highly-acclaimed book on character and positive choices for girls, BeYOUtiful!, which was awarded a National Children's Moonbeam Book Award in recognition as one of the top books on self-esteem for girls and young women. She is also founder of the BeYOUtiful™ Club, a positive role model and mentoring program for amazing girls that empowers them to live extraordinary lives of character and leadership, and to inspire other girls to do the same.

Julie has reached over half a million girls, youth, educators and parents with her life-changing messages. Top leading organizations choose Julie as their trusted speaker and go-to leading authority for their events and programs.

To bring the power of Julie's highly engaging and interactive programs to support your event or conference:

Visit: www.juliespeaks.com

Email: info@juliespeaks.com

Call: 1-800-571-1937